Finding Your
LIFE MISSION

Finding Your
LIFE MISSION

How to Unleash
That Creative Power
and Live With Intention

Naomi Stephan, Ph.D.

STILLPOINT PUBLISHING

Books that explore the expanding frontiers
of human consciousness

For a free catalog or ordering information
write
Stillpoint Publishing, Box 640, Walpole, NH 03608
or call
1-800-847-4014 TOLL FREE
(Continental US, except NH)
1-603-756-9281
(Foreign and NH)

This book is manufactured in the United States of America.

Text design by Irv Perkins Associates, Brattleboro, VT.

Cover design by Bellwether Peers, Peterborough, NH.
Typesetting by NK Graphics, Keene, NH.

Published by Stillpoint Publishing, a division of
Stillpoint International, Inc.

Box 640, Meetinghouse Road, Walpole, NH 03608.

Published simultaneously in Canada by Fitzhenry &
Whiteside Ltd., Toronto.

Library of Congress Catalog Card Number 88-062959
Stephan, Naomi

Finding Your Life Mission
ISBN 0-913299-48-0
9 8 7 6 5 4 3

To Sue for her love and support.
Du bist geschlossen in meinem Herzen.

Sigh for the Divine.
   —Hildegard Von Bingen

LEARN TO THINK LIZARD

Learn to think watercress,
Subtle and crisp.
Learn to see clean, unblinking
Into cool shadows that hide from dust
Of afternoon light.

Learn to think lizard
Slink past the obvious
To the underneath leaf
And there in canny damp twilight
Of cucumber truth
Breathe with your skin
The peace of the rain, the pond, the fern.
   —Sue Moore

"Finding Your Life Mission"/Stephan

Naomi Stephan, Ph.D., is a partner in Stephan/Moore Associates, Inc., of
Santa Monica, Ca. As a public speaker and consultant, she offers five
FINDING YOUR LIFE MISSION™ programs:

- individual consultations
- telephone consultations for people outside the Los Angeles area
- speeches for corporations, non-profit agencies and professional
  organizations
- workshops and week-end seminars
- training programs for qualified individuals who desire certification as a
  FINDING YOUR LIFE MISSION™ instructor in their geographic
  area

Send inquiries to:

Stephan Moore Associates, Inc.
444 Lincoln Blvd., Suite 331
Venice, CA 90291
(213) 399-0657

Contents

Acknowledgments

A book is like a musical composition. It has a creator, but she can only be heard with the help of others. In my case, in addition to Sue, I am grateful to my sister Judith, who spent many hours after a long working day reading (and rereading) the various stages of this manuscript, making valuable editorial and textual suggestions and never failing to include words of encouragement. Thanks go also to Robin Ladd, who gave a certain rigor to the process, challenging me on many concepts and ideas. Posthumous thanks go to Richard Byrne, who understood the urgency of my message and encouraged me to continue my mission of transformation.

I am grateful also to all those people who asked about the progress of the book, listened to me and then gave me fresh perspective on my material. Special thanks go to all my clients, whose path and pilgrimage I was privileged to share.

Last, but by no means least, my thanks are to my parents: my father, who bequeathed to me the beauty of a calling, and who never had a chance to see this book. And to my mother, who has steadfastly believed in me, and whose handwritten note to me I have carried for years in my purse: "Stay happy and optimistic. There is a niche for you in life, you'll find it and you will fit into it perfectly. I love you."

Foreword

If you want to lead a life which expresses your innermost being, if you want to be in consonance with yourself, this book is for you. It doesn't matter where you are coming from. Maybe you haven't the foggiest notion of what your mission is, perhaps you doubt that you even have one, or maybe you need a boost of courage to pursue your own destiny.

All you need is the desire to find your mission. This book gives you the tools to achieve it.

If you want only fame and fortune as a result of this book, look elsewhere. The goal of *Finding Your Life Mission* is for you to develop authenticity, self-trust, centeredness, insight, faithfulness, self-love, creativity, spiritual growth, and most important, realize your destiny. Fame and fortune, on the other hand, can come from living your mission.

Reasons for This Book

Life is difficult if you do not accept—or manifest—your personal mission. My father was an example of someone who did not. He looked upon his ministerial office with enormous reverence, and referred to it as a call coming from a divine source. But, he chose his head over his heart by listening to the voice of "logic." He followed family tradition and became a clergyman like his father, rather than respond to his own passion (= mission) for ancient history and being a professor. Because his mission was unfulfilled, he experienced stress, melancholy, sadness, and depression.

My mother, too, never completely embraced her one true desire—music. Sure, she identified what it was, but failed to manifest it fully in her life. (Does any of this sound familiar to you?) For both my parents, life became tedious instead of tantalizing.

I followed their example for more than twenty years, putting all my energy into pursuing a path that didn't satisfy me. Like my parents, I experienced despair, unhappiness, and anger as proof that something was lacking. In my case, it had meant turning my back on singing and music even though I couldn't bear the pain caused by my abandonment. Because I neglected my uniqueness, I had less of my true self to draw upon for years. (After all, how can you be successful expressing what you aren't?)

Why Mission?

I figured if three intelligent people had missed the boat, there might be a lot of others out there who were experiencing the same pain. Then one day I had an important realization that the concept of a calling applied to life in its totality, not just to the strictly religious interpretation my father had assumed. Everyone had a mission!

That insight became the seed for my private consulting work, and for this book. From my personal experience, I became convinced that most people fail to answer their personal callings fully. Even if they are sick unto death of the life they are leading, they still deny love and commitment to the one who needs it most—themselves. The indicators are everywhere: ignoring a passion for drawing as a youngster, or carrying out what friends want, taking the "practical" route through college (to get that "good" job), marrying because "that's what one is supposed to do," abandoning a career which languishes in the corner of their heart, cancelling a longed-for trip to Europe in favor of a condo on the beach or a bigger house in the suburbs.

Lives are at odds with desires. When a baby cries, it has specific needs: a hug, milk, or perhaps a warm blanket. It's not a condo on the beach that it wants. Yet adults often displace their desires onto a career, money, or a condo on the beach, rather than affirming their need for love, fulfillment, and self-expression.

Further indicators are staying with that stultifying job (or even an okay one) to buy freedom for the future, giving up acting solely to have kids or turning a deaf ear to an inner calling because "it wouldn't pay the rent," living in the city when the country beckons, remaining in a relationship for anyone's sake but your own, or even dying rather than surrendering to the need to cease self-abusive behavior.

The inevitable emotional consequences of a missed mission are discomfort, disappointment, distress, and discouragement, while job failure, addictions, loss of productivity, relationship problems, or disease are the visible symptoms.

Benefits of *Finding Your Life Mission*

After reading this book, you'll be able to access your internal desires. You'll discover a clarity of purpose you hadn't previously known, an ability to live your calling because you'll be able to act in sync with yourself. You'll no longer need to respond to any static from your inner critic or others. You'll know what you are about and your mission will blossom. Life will take on a sensual, pungent, warm—even erotic quality. When my mission began to make "sense" to me, it tasted sweet like cherries, smelled like lily of the valley, sounded like church bells, felt like a Persian cat, and looked like a Venetian Tiepolo sky. You'll learn how to describe and identify your mission in those ways and many more.

With a mission, you'll find that a sense of direction and purpose will permeate your entire being. You'll anticipate what happens next because luck will befall you (the word happen contains the idea of luck), rather than being on the receiving line of "chance." You'll know that opportunity is knocking because now, you hear it. You'll feel a happiness you never knew you were capable of. Most important, you will be the person you were meant to be. What could be more natural than playing your own role in life?

How to Use This Book

This book has a non-linear, multi-faceted approach. You are encouraged to dip into any chapter at whatever point you need to, to take responsibility for your needs. You are encouraged to get a mission notebook, take notes, make comments in the margins. This book is far from fireside reading. It's serious business dealing with the most important thing you'll ever need for your life.

We'll focus on the internal work needed to find your calling, taking you from maintenance and survival thinking to exploration and expansion, from focusing on logic (your shoulds) to a deeper level of what YOU really want in life (your desires).

In Chapters 1–3, we'll examine the concept of Life Mission, discuss your own method of achieving it, and illustrate how creativity will enhance your mission search. In Chapters 4–13 we'll show you ten creative paths to reach your mission. Chapter 14 concludes with a discussion of where to go from here.

My mission in this book is to evoke the feeling that you are a special and unique person. Your life matters. It makes—indeed must make—a difference. Your life must be exciting, optimistic, joyful, energetic, and harmonious. You must express who you are from the depths of your being to invoke and celebrate your creative self in the service of self and humanity.

I want you to say of your life: mission accomplished.

Part One

PAVING THE WAY

Chapter One

Life Mission

We have different gifts. If our gift is preaching let us preach to the limit of our vision. If it is serving others let us concentrate on our service; if it is teaching let us give all we have; and if our gift be the stimulating of the faith of others let us set ourselves to it.

—THE LETTER TO ROME (J. B. PHILLIPS TRANSLATION)

*L*ife is a personal mission. You have a calling which exists **only for you** and which **only you** can fulfill. It takes courage and self-love to answer that inner voice, but being faithful to it is the only way to lead a rewarding life. It's also the most natural way to be. As the Zen master said to his student: "Zen is eating when you are eating." Life is living your personal mission.

Your first obligation is to carry out the mission you are meant for, not what your father, mother, mate, or friends say you should do. Do not let yourself be "should upon!" *No one can go through your life, tell you what it is or how to live it except you.* Your mission will manifest in you when you decide to listen to your heart's desire.

We're talking about self-care here: releasing the need

3

to please others so you take care of yourself! Every one of you has an individual mission to fulfill. Each of you has an individual part to play. There are no substitutes for you, no actors standing in the wings to take your role. And there is no need, or time, to meddle in each other's roles!

Your mission is the most important gift you will ever receive and give in your life. It has only one requirement: that you follow your inner voice. You have no excuses for missing the mark because it's your mark. The ultimate source for your answers is an inside job.

The beauty of discovering your Life Mission is that you get in touch with that special self-imposed assignment only you are qualified to fulfill.

What Is Life Mission?

Life Mission represents the very essence of who you are. It is your very deepest intention—the heartbeat, core, and overall theme which guides your life. It expresses what you are all about. Other words for mission include a calling, a quest, sending, destiny, or assignment.

Once you understand your calling, you learn to connect who you are to what you are doing. Everything makes sense because you do it in the light of your mission. Every task takes on a special meaning, subsumed as it is under this highest heading of your life. A mission, then, provides the context which gives purpose, shape and direction to your entire life.

The "I Have a Dream" speech of Dr. Martin Luther King in Washington expressed his mission: that the different races of this country could live and pray in peace with one another. Everything he did related to that mission, which was, as he put it, to be "a drum major for justice." Likewise your mission dream, whatever it may be, illuminates your way like a beacon. It is truly a "light unto your path," as the Bible puts it.

But What If I Don't Know Yet What My Mission Is?

Some fortunate people (for example, Surgeon General Koop and Isaac Stern), know their mission at an early age. If you despair because you haven't yet found yours, take heart. For many, a realized mission might not come until mid-life, for whatever reason. Anne Morrow Lindbergh made the transformation from poet to world explorer as a grown woman. John Kennedy achieved his mission as a charismatic leader in his forties. Jacqueline Cochran was poor, never knew who her parents were, yet eventually became the first woman to break the sound barrier. Eleanor Roosevelt moved from a subordinate role to a world figure in her later years. And look at Grandma Moses! A mission achieved is never too late

The important thing here is to seek and then carry out your assignment. Awaken your own discovery process so that you can own and walk your true path, just as countless other courageous people have done.

Why Mission and Not Career?

A mission can take various forms: a career, an avocation, a hobby, a pastime, a passion or anything in between. That is why this book emphasizes mission rather than career, because Life Mission goes far beyond simply what you do for a living. The term Life Mission refers to who you are and what your purpose is in life. A career is what you do. Mission is the melody,

5

career is the musical instrument you play it on. It's just one of the many possibilities of expressing your melody.

What Are Some Examples of Life Mission?

Perhaps your assignment is to explore the polar ice caps, like Admiral Byrd. Maybe it is to protect consumers like Ralph Nader or to be part of a creative duo such as Gertrude Stein and Alice B. Toklas.

Missions can be humble as well as grand. A mission could be the greening of Los Angeles through planting trees (the goal of the L.A. organization Tree People); dealing with sick babies, as does Charles Ballard, a 62-year-old registered nurse; or Ila Loetscher's passion for sheltering injured and sick sea turtles. Perhaps it is to keep the floors of the local hospital sparkling, to give people the best taxi ride they have ever had or to make the most elaborate and biggest soap bubbles. (These are all missions of everyday folks I have noted.) Any mission is valid so long as it expresses the talent, gift, and desire *you hold most dear.*

The Missionary Spirit

Every mission requires courage and commitment. People with a mission are dauntless, tenacious souls. They have answered their inner voice, taken risks and responded when opportunity knocked. Their lives seem to say: "I know who I am and where I want to be, and nothing is going to stand between me and my destiny. I refuse to hold back or to deprive myself of my purpose." Mission seekers may have battled institutions, State, society, relatives, parents, and even mates to fulfill their calling. They persevere without asking permission from others and accept responsibility for the outcome. And you can do that, too.

From Mission Impossible to Possible

In the old TV series called "Mission: Impossible," the main character was always given an "impossible" assignment to perform. "Your mission, if you choose to accept it . . ." was the stock statement each week. The viewers *knew* the lead character was going to accept that mission, and there was never any doubt he would succeed. That's a good message right there.

Let's compare that TV series with the concept of mission:

1. You get your Life Mission from yourself. Unlike the show, your assignment comes from within. *Your first assignment is to discover what has always been there.* "But," you may protest, "I need to pay for my exotic cockatoo, see the kids through school, keep up my standard of living, join the country club," etc. Anything else but "This is what I need to do." The creative web that you spin, like that of the spider, must come from within. Manifesting your Life Mission is like weaving your own special web. There's no other pattern quite like yours.

2. Your mission is possible. It would be the quintessential cosmic joke for you to want something you couldn't fulfill. If it's your heart's desire, you can achieve it.

Farmer Gene

Gene, a lanky bean pole of a fellow from northern Iowa, remembered applying for management positions

7

after leaving graduate school. Believing he should get a "real" job, he sent out applications for positions he didn't want. From the start he knew that these positions weren't his calling. Like a kid pretending to enjoy school when he'd rather be outdoors, he was just going through the motions.

The problem wasn't his qualifications. Gene had an MBA with honors from the University of Minnesota. But those positions didn't intersect properly with his Life Mission. He had plenty of clues: making himself feel at home with old family photos, his grandma's quilts, playing his Dad's harmonica, or taking walks in the countryside with the dog. And, every vacation he went back to the family farm, where he looked after the livestock and checked to see the condition of the soil and property. "As a child," he related, "I was really attached to the animals. I nursed many a bird's broken wing and talked to the cows during milking."

Gene was at heart a country boy. He felt about as comfortable in a business suit as a unicorn does in a water bed store. But to please his father, he had gone off to the city to "make a name for himself" (that is, for his family), by taking a 9–5 job. He was blind to the clues.

After ten years of working indoors, Gene came in for some advice. It took only a short while for him to see the light. He simply began to acknowledge the clues. Even his checks had rural scenes on them! He returned to the area he loved and bought some land. Never mind that farms were folding left and right around him. He answered his call of being a caretaker of the land. And, his MBA came in handy. (Nothing is ever lost.) Gene combined farming and consulting for local businesses and farmers.

For a mission to be truly yours, desire and ability need to be in harmony. Like Gene, you may con yourself into thinking you want to pursue a particular path, but that deception won't work forever. It never does. The mission search requires honesty and determination

3. You have the choice to accept your Life Mission. It's yours for the taking. To be yourself is quite simple. Who else is better qualified to be you? What if someone decided to take over *your role* in life? Would you sit back calmly without comment? You'd probably find that person can't really be you as well as you can. It's your decision to accept your role and act according to *your true nature.*

4. Your Life Mission is unique. If you have been conditioned by herd thinking to be a part of the pack, to emphasize sameness and minimize the differences, it's difficult to identify the unique part of yourself.

What is unique about *you?* Statements such as "I'm a mother of three children" or, "I like people" or, "I have an aardvark in my backyard" don't count because they refer to something external rather than a special quality in *you.* Focus on a characteristic that has always been inseparable from you.

When I asked Jim, a scientist, about his mission, he said he had the unique capacity to know just how things interconnected. He declared at age seven: "The bombing of Hiroshima is bad for people and it will hurt the fish, too!" For him, caring about the planet and making connections between events shaped his unique mission as an environmental activist/biologist.

Sometimes I Feel Like a Missionless Child

Many people have neglected their mission. They remain, like the man in Kafka's parable *Before the Law*, languishing at the entrance gate to their own space.

What might keep you from embracing the thing that is most yours? You may simply need the concepts and tools to gain entry to your mission. Perhaps you're just afraid. Or, you might need encouragement. Maybe you feel the years lost will be too painful, that others will disapprove of your decisions or you'll lose what you've gained if you change course now.

But as the song lyric goes: "So how could you lose what you've never owned?" What do you profit if you've gained the whole world but lost your own mission?

Whatever has kept you off course, you can change *now*! Denying your destiny is the ultimate self-denial. Remember that:

- there are clues that your mission has always been within you.
- missed missions can—and must—be found.
- you can break through any barriers to your mission.
- responding to a calling, and not fame and fortune, are the measure of happiness.

There are no short cuts to figuring out your life: no instant this and immediate that. Look at all the "how-to" books out there that offer easy solutions and quick fixes. And, the national passion for alternative ways to get high through drugs, sex, or fads is an example of trying to get to the top without doing the work. You reach your peak if you are willing to climb for it. That's why this book is serious business, not just fireside reading with popcorn and the cat.

Mission: Getting Down to Business

The concept of mission has long been used in business. Most corporations have a mission statement in their

by-laws. Even a local golf course has a mission statement pasted onto the starter's window!

A mission statement answers two basic questions:
What benefits to humanity are we giving through our
product or service? What is our responsibility to the
world at large? Whether a company produces chariots,
cherries, chimneys, or provides services such as career
counseling, catering or cleaning, it needs a clear purpose that goes *beyond the product itself.*

Companies that fulfill their missions are immediately
recognizable. Think of a shop where you like to do
business. Chances are that this business is doing well
and is popular with its customers, because it's a place
with a clearly identified purpose.

A good example of such a company is Nordstrom.
It has such a fine reputation for customer service that
people flock to its doors. It attracts people because it
is one place where customers' needs come first.

In one instance, a Nordstrom salesperson spent a
considerable amount of time bringing various sizes and
styles of clothes back to the dressing room, allowing
the customer to make her decisions without having to
get dressed again and run out to the showroom.

When the customer couldn't find the coat she
wanted, the saleswoman went to a rival store, bought
it for her, charging her only the actual price of the coat.
You can bet that saleswoman gained a loyal customer!
Nordstrom's mission goes beyond selling clothes. It is
to serve the customers and give them what they need.
Business has known for a long time that a clear and
beneficial mission gets results!

11

Self-Help Exercises for Your Life Mission Search

Just because you have a Life Mission doesn't mean that it will be self-evident. You need to do the inner work of listening to yourself. First, you need to be very clear. Just who is the person looking for this mission?

Exercise 1.1: I AM.

Each of us is a singular, one-of-a-kind mixture of talents, experience, and background. The parts are like the warp and woof of your unique fabric. On separate pieces of paper, put I AM at the top of each page. Then list one thing, such as: I AM a daughter, student, tennis enthusiast. Now what does your particular set of ingredients tell you about yourself? For example, a sample list from a client:

I AM: woman, speaker of French, traveler, reader of autobiographies, soap opera addict, pillowcase collector, plant lover, dancer, American, golfer (in low 80's). This person actually started to investigate new ideas for beautifying golf courses—in France!

By seeing yourself as unique, you can respond to your particular gift within. Your mission expresses a specific role, and your uniqueness is the tool with which you can carry it out.

Exercise 1.2: TALK TO YOUR MISSION AS A LOVER.

Imagine your mission as a person you love who is sitting across from you. See it as a close relationship of yours. Feel it as an energy, a spirit, a part of you. You want to clear the air about problems in the relationship. This is the time to be candid with your partner. (You don't need to know what your specific mission is for now.)

a) Tell your mission everything you appreciate about it. Address the mission as "you." For example: "I love you because you give me a feeling of power and energy whenever I embrace you." "I get a rush when we're in sync with each other."

b) Now tell your mission what you expect from it. Be candid! What do you need from your mission? For example: "I want you to encourage me and let me know when I am neglecting you."

c) Tell your mission in what ways your needs have not yet been met. What do you miss in your relationship? "I need quiet time to talk with you."

d) Reverse the role now, and become your mission. As mission, you are going to talk to YOU. Repeat a–c. Tell YOU what YOU AS MISSION expect, and what you as mission are not getting. "You never spend enough time with me. You leave me last in your plans."

e) Analyze this scene as if you had heard two lovers discussing their relationship. What is your assessment of their problem? How well do they get along? What's the prognosis for their relationship?

13

What does each party need to do to improve the relationship?

f) Finally, write your mission a love letter. If you find you have been afraid to get too intimate with your mission, put your feelings down in letter form. Say everything you feel. Do not be shy about role-playing your mission, too! It can give you a lot of insight about your relationship to it.

Exercise 1.3: *DESCRIBE HOW YOUR LIFE MISSION LOOKS OR FEELS.*

Use any metaphor, image, or analogy you can think of. You are developing your own personal mythology. Put as much sensory detail in it as possible. It might go something like this: "My mission looks like a huge medieval castle on a hill with turrets and flags waving in the summer breeze," or, "My mission feels like that of Persephone, travelling back and forth between the underworld and here. I am a traveler like her connecting the two worlds of the spiritual and the worldly."

What kinds of things are evoked in you when you read your description? Put them down in a Life Mission notebook. Add to this description from time to time. Notice if any pattern or theme recurs. (Mine always had musical references.)

Exercise 1.4: IMAGINE YOU WROTE YOUR LIFE SCRIPT.

You are not a victim. Start seeing your family as an asset. By focusing on the role you played in your family, you'll discover how your particular family configuration *enabled* you to be who you are and how it helped mold your mission.

Rewrite your parental script. Imagine you chose your parents. What would have prompted you to pick them and the number of siblings you have? Why did you elect to be born at a particular time and place in history? What can you learn from your chosen lifestyle, relatives, and family members?

1. Julia, a free-lance journalist, chose a family in which there was a high degree of intellectual energy. She got lots of things ready-made: educated parents, intellectual stimulation, and lively conversation. But her family had difficulty expressing feelings. When Julia became a journalist, she found her home life gave her depth of critical analysis, the ability to think and converse. But perhaps most important was her compassion for people who avoided feelings. In therapy she worked through her self-expression blocks. Now she is ingenious at getting people she interviews to express themselves, knowing firsthand how difficult it was for herself to do just that.

2. Mike felt being gay was a disadvantage. How could he have wanted this sexual preference? He began to look at his "liability" as an asset and discovered that his sexuality allowed him to see things from both sides of the coin. (Other minorities will understand this.) Mike's gift was the ability to solve problems. He was

15

especially talented at coming up with alternative view-
points which he had no trouble doing because he was
living differently than the "norm." He began to look
at his sexuality not as a curse but as an opportunity. It
allowed him to see things from a different perspective
because his life was free of conventional choices.

In your journal, list the reasons why your life circumstances required that you lived where and when you
did. State why you needed each close family member
for growth in your life.

Clues to Your Mission

Everyone likes clues. Here are some vital tips to help
identify when you are on the right track with your
mission.

Clue #1: Know your passion and enjoyment. Jean,
a real estate broker, was forever puttering in her garden
and helping friends with theirs. She would habitually
stop to look at new landscape designs and she owned
a collection of books on interior design. But hard as it
is to believe, until Jean observed what she actually
liked doing—creating beauty through nature—she didn't
recognize the clues! The body always responds to right
action and right thought by giving you energy. Look
for times when you feel that energy. Most often it will
be evident as passion or enjoyment. When you're on
track, you'll catch yourself feeling enthusiastic, moved,
and alive. Let's look at Brenda's example:

Drawing on Your Skills

A very discerning Southern woman with an investigative bent, Brenda was heading into her forties with
a sense of being totally off-base with her mission. A

16

native of Georgia, Brenda loved those old Southern mansions and the sense of history in her environment. She lamented the decay of those buildings whenever she read about it (clue!).

Brenda knew what she was interested in, but she was having a difficult time translating it into practical terms. She spent a lot of effort in finding reasons why she should not pursue her mission of aesthetic preservation. A French language teacher, she secretly wanted to use her artistic talents to restore and recover art. But she insisted there was no way to express exactly what she wanted because it was so rare.

She told me of an incident on a plane flight in which a fellow passenger described a rather unusual passion. He made underwater drawings of archaeological sites. "Wouldn't you love to do that?" I asked. She literally rose up in her chair, her eyes brightened, and she cried, "YES!" Then she slumped back down and sighed, "But there isn't a market for such an unusual thing." For a brief moment, Brenda had experienced a clue of passion.

What would that passenger be doing now if he had limited himself with such thinking?

What *are* you passionate about? What gives you energy? Include any items from the past. Pay attention to those clues which tell you what YOU want in your mission. Even if the enjoyment is for a fleeting moment, make note of it! Observe what you catch yourself enjoying (it isn't always obvious.) Sometimes a purpose can stare you in the face and you won't recognize it, but by acknowledging your passions, you can see your mission more clearly.

Get out your mission journal and write down examples. Don't stop to analyze or censor them. Just write down your passions and enjoyments as fast as you can

until you can't think of any more. Add any that occur
to you over time. After you have a sizable list (say 10–
20 items), look for the clues, common threads, and
experiences that weave through your list.

Do you enjoy physical things? Mental things? Outdoor things? Solitary things? Things involving nature?
Animals? Position yourself to encounter more of your
passions and enjoyments by seeking out environments
where you will unleash those feelings. For example, if
you like animals, go to a zoo. If you like mountains,
go hiking. If you like children, go to a playground!

Clue #2: Monitor your aches and pains. When
you fail to respond to your inner wisdom, you'll feel
specific emotional and physical reactions resulting from
that neglect. Your mission will nestle somewhere in
your body and reveal its presence through aches and
pains. Consult your body and let it tell you what the
problem is.

Keep track of those aches and pains. When and
where do they flare up? Identify any sad experiences
you have had and where the pain was located. What
were the circumstances of the experience? How did
you react? What caused the pain to stop, if indeed it
did?

Wood That Catherine Could

Catherine, a recent divorcée, first felt the pain when
she worked on the doors of her house. The process of
sanding, staining, and varnishing wood brought back
memories of construction work which she had done
just after high school. She had always loved woodwork,
but had been talked out of it because it wasn't "lady-
like" enough. If you asked her any question about
wood she'd talk your ear off.

18

But it wasn't until she began to build the kids a tree house that her previous neglect of wood really hit her. She developed a pain in her chest, so much so that she thought the physical exertion might be causing a strain on her heart. The doctor couldn't find anything wrong. (It was precisely the opposite, of course. *Neglect* had caused a strain on her heart.) She began to spend as much time with wood as possible. The pain stopped when she satisfied her need to use wood for play and leisure. And, she made it profitable besides: Catherine started a woodworking business designing and building children's tree- and playhouses.

Clue #3: Look for rewards. You're never punished for following your path. Some form of reward will always occur. Something positive will happen. It might come in the form of a gift, such as a trip to a foreign country from a relative. Or it might be a sudden loan to continue graduate study. It might be something quite non-material, such as an insight, a day free of anxiety or a call from a long-lost friend.

Last year I bought new stereo speakers for the first time in 17 years. I needed them for my reawakening musical self. The first time I listened to these new speakers, I experienced the rush I had felt with the first set. In the next day's mail I received a check from an unexpected source which was for the *exact amount of the speakers*. Coincidence? Or a reward?

For a three-week period focus on doing what you really like for as much time as you can possibly spare (see **Clue #1** for ideas). During this time, write down every positive, unusual, or unexpected thing that happens to you. They will be your rewards!

Nancy, an accountant, was wrestling with making some changes in her life. She decided to work on a project for the homeless and reduced her accounting practice. She also decided to pursue additional schooling, even if she didn't yet know what. During a period of three weeks, she kept a list and totalled more than fifty rewards. They included:

- a workshop flyer addressed to a previous occupant at *her* address, which gave Nancy the answer about a direction she should take in her schooling.
- an unexpected referral for a new account with a huge commission.
- permission from her landlady to keep a stray (homeless!) cat.

There are always rewards for carrying out your Life Mission. They may be invisible at the time but you will get them. Move closer to your path and you will be showered with support

Clue #4: Recognize your fears. Fear is a friendly reminder that you may be running from the very thing you love. Fear often arises when you refuse to face your mission. Look at Dan:

Father Dan

Dan, a CEO in a large financial institution, was so terrified about dealing with his Life Mission (nurturing young people), that he actually cringed whenever he said any word remotely connected to it. It was as if saying the word would cause lightning to strike. He feared what he loved. Dan was especially interested in helping kids with their financial planning.

Danny had spent twenty years escaping his desire to be a financial nurturer for youngsters. He thought it wasn't manly, and couldn't see any way to make a living from it. Danny resisted going to the local youth center and offering financial advice to teenagers. Finally he squarely faced his passion to nurture others and was rewarded with a new job and a leadership position in a local youth club.

He volunteered his services now and then to youth groups and his face would flush as he told me about it. "Those kids actually thanked me for helping them set up a budget," he said as tears welled up in his eyes. "Maybe they'll have a future a little freer of anxiety than I did at their age."

a) Complete the sentence: "I'm afraid of _____ _____." List every fear individually, no matter how silly, trivial, or huge. "I'm afraid of coughing in movie theaters" is just as important to acknowledge as "I'm afraid of death."

b) Then on a separate page, turn those fear statements into desires by completing the words "I want _____." For example, "I want to sit through a movie quietly" or "I want to accept my own mortality."

c) For each desire example put the result that you want. For example, "I want to go a movie once a week" or "I want to write my will calmly" might be things you would do if fear hadn't prevented it for so long. Just rewriting your fears will encourage you to address them through action and get moving in the direction you want. Now get started on one example!

Clue #5: What do you want to learn? When you want to find out about something, it shows that a desire is awakened in you. What stimulates your curiosity?

Get a college catalogue and page through it, picking out five courses you'd take without worrying about time, money, or skills. Write all those items down in your notebook.

Then look for clues about things you want to know more about. Some items on the list may even surprise you. One client's list included astronomy, which provided a missing piece of the puzzle—where to relocate to fulfill her mission. She realized that she needed to move to a Western state with wide open skies to raise people's consciousness about the gentle treatment of animals.

The teacher teaches what the teacher needs to know. Mission and learning mirror each other like reflecting pools. After all, Mozart wanted to learn more about music and Leonardo da Vinci about the human figure (and not vice versa). What you want to learn gives you clues about your mission.

Gentle Joe

Joe, a 45-year-old politician with a tough, street-wise exterior yet gentle interior, began to sense his Life Mission: making the world a safer place for children. When Joe was a young boy, he would regularly get beaten up on the way to school. Later (still not knowing the reason), he decided to become a policeman. He was interested in learning about crime detection, self-defense techniques, and breaking patterns of violence in school children

Joe became a police commissioner. It was not until *twenty years later* that Joe realized why he had entered law enforcement. (Remember, your Life Mission can often be staring you in the face and you won't always see it.) Joe made a further transition having studied for a degree in political science in order to continue his mission in politics.

List up to ten things you want to learn more about. What is it about each of them that intrigues you? Who can help you get more information or training in this area? What does your list reveal about your Life Mission?

Clue #6: Who are your heroes? Think of the books you used to read as a child or the ones your parents read to you. Who are the people, fictitious or real, living or dead, whom you admired? Maybe you kept a scrapbook or clippings on your heroes. Maybe you went back to the city library again and again to reread that one story about the aviator Amelia Earhart or the baseball player Jackie Robinson. They will tell you a lot about the person you want to be. The kind of people they were, the situations they found themselves in, and the results they got will give you insights into your own directions.

Santa Barbara

Barbara identified with Saint Joan of Arc. She recognized that her need to be a crusader, an activist, and a famous woman had long been languishing. Her interests were in science and writing and her heroes included Jacques Cousteau, and Merian, an eighteenth-century female German explorer. Barbara wanted to learn more about how to write non-fiction and scientific articles creatively. She wanted to direct her crusading spirit in the service of the environment by using her scientific background and writing ability to support crusades in these causes.

Write down three heroes you identified with and list the qualities or deeds you admired in them. Identify those traits which YOU would like to have. In what

context (that is, setting, area, work place, geographic
location, etc.) could these qualities best be put to use?

Life Mission Statement

It's time for you to take the first step toward describing
your Life Mission. We'll begin this way. Use only one
word per space:

I AM _____.

I am most me when I am _____ (state
of being).

I enjoy_____ (interest area) most,
and I feel it most intensely when I am _____
_____ (activity or environment).

I tend to fear _____ most.

It pains me in anger _____ (area of body)
when I do not _____ (activity).

I most want to learn about _____.

My hero is _____.

I was born into my family to experience _____.

My mission needs _____ (quality) from
me.

My mission feels/looks like _____
_____ (description).

My mission is inseparable from my talent of _____
_____.

Build from here by adding your own sentences. In
the following chapters you will be encircling your Life

Mission by focusing on it from different angles. In fact, the goal of every exercise and this book is for you to clarify, identify, and live the mission you have.

Is your mission to make people laugh? To be an inspiration to the schoolchildren of New Concord? To bring music to the disadvantaged? Or does it have to do with creating something from cardboard, recording the lives of elephants, manufacturing rubber bands, or to educate people about the beauty and ecology of the Grand Canyon (all real missions I have culled from various sources)?

The *nature* of a mission can be anything. The important thing is that it reflects who you are and makes a positive contribution to yourself and the world.

Your Life Mission is, in the striking poem "On His Blindness," by John Milton, "that one Talent which is death to hide." It's the gift you were endowed with. Unwrap it! You have the answer to your calling within you; it just needs to become part of your conscious awareness. There is no better gift.

Chapter Two

Mission à la Mode

*C*heck the category which describes the way you most like to do things:

— I take charge to get things done
— I motivate others to get things done
— I cooperate with others to get things done
— I make sure to get things done with quality and standards

Are you here to make a splash or work quietly? Do you prefer to work with people or with facts and things? Do you want to make your mark on stage or behind the scenes? Do you want to move mountains or inspire people to move them?

Each of you runs your life in a specific way to meet

your goals and needs. We'll call that your primary mode (PM). Your PM is distinctive to you. Life Mission expresses who you are, and PM expresses *in what manner* you prefer to achieve your mission.

When your mission and PM are congruent, you can be more effective, more creative, and self-actualizing. You can integrate who you are with what you do. And, by learning to better recognize and appreciate your PM, you'll be able to channel your energy wisely and maximize its use in the service of your mission.

Like your mission, your PM is a "comfort zone." It should match you and not the other way around. When your mission is out-of-phase with your PM, it creates tension, distress, and rarely leads to productive efforts.

Your PM reflects who you are when you are acting most naturally. As soon as you recognize that you like to do things a certain way, and understand how to use that knowledge appropriately, you can risk accepting the mission which matches your PM (it always will). The purpose of this chapter is to give you insight into how you like to do things, and how to make that PM work for you in the service of your mission.

Doing What Comes Naturally

You function better when you can be and act in self-awareness and in harmony with your PM. One person's PM is not necessarily another's. But, you say, wouldn't I naturally use my own PM? Not necessarily. I stress in this book that we often defer to others on how we should run our lives.

For example, my father and I had different ways of accomplishing our goals, and each way was valid in its own right. For him, sermons had to be rehearsed in

27

the study on Thursdays from 9–12, and be exactly three and a half typewritten pages in length.

For many years I used a PM more like my father's, writing out all my lecture notes and rehearsing them the night before. (He was an Analyzer.) I knew how many pages an hour's lecture required and even practiced those lectures while walking around! I deliberated and obsessed about things. Would we discuss the Rococo Period before Spring break or after? It didn't work. I was unconsciously trying to pattern my behavior after my father's PM. (I am a Motivator.)

Later I realized that to be effective, I had to be more spontaneous. I also had to realize my mission, and any part thereof (= speeches) in the same way.

Why You Must Be Aware of Your PM

In a hilarious scene in "I Love Lucy," Lucille Ball portrayed a harried worker who was trying to keep up with an assembly line moving faster and faster. The conveyor belt won. Perhaps you have felt in that position on occasion. No matter what you do, life wants it done faster or differently. You feel helpless to meet others' demands. And then, like the character Lucille Ball played, you end up thinking any failure is your fault.

Misunderstanding your PM can cause you to negate your own behavior. The clearer you get about your own PM and the more comfortable you feel about yourself, the more you can work on a mission *your way*. Let's look at Alan and Marilyn:

Alan Accepts

Alan, a free-lance writer, was in a funk. His mission, to inspire people to political awareness through writ-

28

ing, was faltering. A lanky man with broad shoulders and a shock of blond hair falling into his eyes, he seemed about to fall apart as he sat in my office shuffling through his briefcase to find his portfolio. Alan's business was also in a state of chronic chaos. Unpaid bills and invoices fluttered among his written work.

Whenever Alan did proofreading, correcting, and editing of material, he felt a certain heaviness. Now Alan thought he was really a detail-oriented person; after all, a person who writes must be organized, right? When his feature article appeared in a magazine with the caption "General arrived uninformed and ready for action," Alan realized he had to do something.

Awareness and acceptance of his PM helped Alan act more in sync with his mission. He had figured his frequent mistakes were a character flaw, rather than low priorities. Frustration over his disorganization was taking away from his ability to write effectively (part of his PM). He set about getting a proofreader and a bookkeeper instead of knocking himself out with something he wasn't good at. Why try for excellence doing things he didn't like when others performed that service so much better? His commissions and his self-esteem increased.

Magic in Hollywood

After analyzing her PM, Marilyn, a soft-spoken New Englander with elegant demeanor, realized why she didn't like details, formal suits, working in structured ways, and "toeing the line." (She was a Doer.) Yet this was what her position in a city agency "demanded" of her. She could also no longer accept being the dutiful employee, especially since she was older than her bosses. The atmosphere at the agency was grim and devoid of humor. To vent her frustration, Marilyn

29

would wait for the next vacation where she could dream of her mission (to be an urban sorcerer).

I asked Marilyn to describe how she would spend a typical work day if she could design it her way. Her PM took on an entirely different look. "In a Hollywood office I'd develop new ideas for designing streets which would show people a new way of experiencing their city," she recounted excitedly. She wanted to be her own boss, and acknowledge the adventurer self she always was. "I don't know why I didn't see this before, but I want to be a big splash, not a tiny drop." Now she is working on a city project dear to her heart, but in her own way.

Marilyn felt she was incompetent and wasting time, Alan thought he was sloppy. Marilyn realized that an aesthetic, urban atmosphere of unsupervised creativity was crucial to her emotional and mental health, while Alan needed an uncluttered environment to create his essays.

Exercise 2.1: BEING WRITE ON

Take a pen and write your signature as if you were writing a check. Better yet, take out your checkbook and make it out to Naomi Stephan. (Just kidding!) Now take your non-preferred hand, and write your signature again. Compare the two. Which one looks better? Went faster? Was easier? More efficient? The signature you wrote with your preferred hand, of course. How many times in the last hundred checks did you use your non-preferred hand? Probably never, and for good reason. Your PM, like your mission, makes life easier, gets results, works faster, and looks better. Right? Why not start using it more consciously!

Getting Conscious of Your PM

In list #1 put check marks beside those words which best characterize you, and total them up. The column with the highest total will be the PM which matches you most.

Doer	Motivator
_____ bold	_____ generous
_____ strong-willed	_____ enthusiastic
_____ decisive	_____ influential
_____ competitive	_____ gullible
_____ self-assured	_____ humorous
_____ tension producer	_____ imaginative
_____ pragmatic	_____ charming
_____ blunt	_____ emotional
_____ tough	_____ self-promoting
_____ impatient	_____ impulsive
_____ dominating	_____ manipulative
_____ cold	_____ dramatic
_____ action-oriented	_____ trusts a lot
_____ self-starter	_____ high contact person
_____ accepts challenge	_____ uses intuition
_____ likes risks	_____ likes persuasion
_____ forceful opinions	_____ likes fun jobs
_____ disciplined, quick	_____ likes to motivate
_____ works on hunches	_____ dislikes details
_____ accepts challenges	_____ visionary

Total: _____   _____

31

Stabilizer

_____ understanding
_____ responsive
_____ agreeable
_____ calm
_____ supportive
_____ dependable
_____ traditional
_____ low key
_____ team player
_____ predictable
_____ loyal
_____ thorough
_____ good listener
_____ logical
_____ sticks to procedure
_____ work in small groups
_____ likes structure
_____ quiet in meetings
_____ methodical
_____ traditional

Total: _____

Analyzer

_____ conventional
_____ organized
_____ orderly
_____ unresponsive
_____ indecisive
_____ exacting
_____ orderly
_____ restrained
_____ critical
_____ disciplined
_____ meticulous
_____ proper
_____ evaluates
_____ works alone
_____ slow-paced
_____ non-verbal
_____ business-like
_____ respects facts
_____ problem solver
_____ likes clarity

_____

My PM is _____.

Your PM choice should match your answer from the beginning of the chapter.

Descriptions of Each PM

The following descriptions will give you further clarification and information on each PM. Read about

32

yours first, then look at the others. You have scores in all categories, and you use all styles at some time or another, but for our purposes here, concentrate on identifying your individual PM. Remember, we're not judging actions here. Rather, we're describing ways persons of a particular mode *prefer to act* to meet their needs.

Doers

Doers get things done fast. I recognize a Doer client when they ask me right off, with eyes screwed up and fingers tapping impatiently on the chair, "How long is this process going to take?"

Doers enjoy challenge, risk, and obstacles. They like to go out on a limb, especially where there's trouble involved. Doers seek dissonance and thrive on conflict. As one put it to me: "I can't stand a job in which nothing happens. Give me a good fight and I'm all set to go."

Doers rarely mix emotions with tasks. If people don't perform and someone has to be terminated, Doers will take care of that job without flinching. They want to tell the rest of the world what to do and take responsibility for the results. Well, someone needs to be daring enough to risk achieving what they say they are going to!

But, if something demands incubation or deliberation, DON'T ask a Doer to wait. On the other hand, if an instant decision is needed, let the Doer handle it.

If you are a Doer, you take decisive steps when everyone else runs around wringing their hands. You probably have your own work space but are rarely in it (and it looks that way, too). In bridge, you bid first and count your points later.

Things that suit your results-oriented PM are those

33

with heavy take-charge responsibility and fast dead-lines. You like to cut through things and get down to business. You are competitors who like nothing better than to be #1 (remember Marilyn). You don't cry over spilled milk or get emotionally involved in the process. You have a strong sense of purpose, of self, and you are a person who cares about what is going on now, rather than the future.

Incidentally, you might find yourself saying: "So what? I know all these things." Remember, you Doers tend to see yourselves as the model of human behavior.

Dot the Doer

Dorothy, a stately woman of thirty-five, had long kept herself in low profile jobs. Seeking out a change of direction from her manufacturing sales rep position in Kansas, she had abruptly moved to Los Angeles. In a PM workshop, Dorothy "discovered" she was a classic Doer. "So what?" she quipped (quick confirmation that the analysis was right).

Dorothy was in transition and planned to have a new job in a new field (human resources) within the next two weeks. (Dorothy was always ten steps ahead of everyone.) Doers do things fast, and sure enough, Dorothy got her new job in record time. I called her and asked how it was going, "Oh," she said, "I'm angry I have to go to work at 5 A.M." "Why?" I asked. "I have to get there by 6 A.M. to make sure nobody gets ahead of me!" was her reply.

I told Dorothy she could continue to leave the house angry, or realize that it was in the nature of her PM to want to be ahead and that she could leave early for work at peace with herself if she took responsibility for her competitive approach.

Dorothy's understanding has led to better perfor-mance because now she arrives at work ready for action rather than being angry and hostile. Her colleagues began to find Dorothy easier to work with. First thing you know, she was presenting a seminar for her company. Doers know only one direction: up. She is moving toward her mission of communicating better performance on the job.

Doers must have a high key mission. It must be a headline edition which requires power and commands recognition. You need to make things happen fast. You must champion a cause and challenge complacency. You are a born rebel for the good of humanity. You must have a leading position to accomplish what you need.

Friendly advice for Doers:

1) incubate ideas, (*be* more, *act* less)
2) weigh evidence more carefully
3) listen to the advice of others
4) inject more warmth and feeling into your relations with others

Motivators

Motivators are the show people of the quartet. Always on stage, emotional, witty, and fast thinking, they want to be like the Pied Piper of Hamelin, inspiring people toward a common goal. If someone is needed to promote ideas or make a product or person look good, Motivators are the best choice. They are consummate salespeople and can wax poetic about toothbrushes, dog collars, table salt or cemetery plots.

Motivators love a pleasant, aesthetic non-business-like atmosphere. They would prefer to do their work

35

in a local café rather than in a stuffy office. When playing bridge, they don't always have their cards arranged properly in suits, but they are creative bidders. If you like to make speeches, be on stage, go out in public, or give presentations of any kind, you're a Motivator. You can be counted on to be friendly, charming, and enthusiastic even under the worst circumstances. Highly reactive, you are likely to flare up easily and dramatize any situation. Tremors become earthquakes when you feel vulnerable. Whereas Doers can forget painful situations fast, you can keep grudges long after everyone else has forgotten what the issue was.

While Doers can work alone, you Motivators depend on other people for emotional support and approval. You wither when people don't respond, and find it difficult to be critical or disciplined. You are the harmony seekers, avoiding conflict, desiring agreement.

A Motivator friend of mine gets great pleasure out of devising funny phone messages to delight his customers. An inveterate ham, he gets people to call just to hear the latest in witty puns. As you can imagine, any phone conversation with this fellow is bound to spark a series of laughs. Motivators do things with gusto.

Activist Alex

In the first session with Alex I could barely get a word in edgewise (typical with Motivators). A good-natured, jovial, winsome man, Alex had spent the last few years in the entertainment industry working as a producer in Hollywood. In this job, Alex was able to explore much of his talent for writing and communication. His marriage was stable, the future looked bright, everything on the surface looked rosy.

But he knew something wasn't right. The old fire he had felt in the sixties as a political activist leading marches had just never surfaced again. He also longed to go back to those areas of the world in which he had travelled in his late twenties. Now he felt stuck, stodgy, out of step with himself and unable to find an outlet for his energy

Alex had spent a year coming up with hundreds of ideas, but he rejected each one as a pipe dream. His present job often left him feeling alone and unappreciated, and his ideas were often discounted. The pressure of the industry sapped Alex's strength for motivational work. He missed the college-age kids he used to work with and the causes he had fought for.

Alex had a pattern of doing things only halfway before going on to the next item. Like many Motivators, he thought he needed to have it all, not understanding that when he had what he wanted, he had it all. As soon as he recognized that he needed to be out there with the troops leading them on, and that he needed a cause to focus on, he finally began to get a glimpse of his mission. He returned to his sixties activism self, twenty years wiser, and put it in the service of teaching.

Alex demonstrates that Motivators are masterful at creative ways to do things and use quick-thinking methods to get something done, but need help in follow-through.

If you are a Motivator, you need to be surrounded, loved, and nourished by people, contact, and applause. That's why you are the performers of the group. You must be visionary and instill people with enthusiasm. You are missionaries with dreams. You love to generate ideas, and come up with more ways to do things than you can use in a lifetime. When no one can think of a new way to do something, or all the ideas seem stale, you get people unstuck.

Your mission needs to involve the stimulation, motivation, and inspiration of people by using your creativity and talents to the common good. You need to use your ideas for future change, and to create an atmosphere of true harmony.

Friendly advice for Motivators:

1) check impulsive behavior
2) avoid manipulating with emotions
3) organize your priorities and
4) work on completing what you start

Stabilizers

Someone once said that Doers and Motivators get raises for what they SAY they do, and Stabilizers and Analyzers for what they ACTUALLY do. Stabilizers are the rocks of Gibraltar, the cool, calm, collected folks who put everyone at ease and make life bearable. Stabilizers are friendly people who prefer being around similar types, although not in such large groups as the Motivator. Stabilizers are sincere, loyal, and cooperative. They are excellent team players. They do not like to rock the boat but prefer to work in a careful, thorough way without sudden changes.

I once had a secretary who was a Stabilizer. I couldn't expect her to initiate things but when I gave directives she carried them out. She had a fantastic routine and followed through on everything I asked. I could count on giving her many things to do because she would decide the method of getting them all done. A Motivator would try to work on them all at once, and a Doer secretary would last only as long as it took her to revamp the entire office.

One of my clients, Dora, refused to acknowledge that she was a Stabilizer. (Unlike Doers, Stabilizers often have trouble accepting their PM.) I asked how long she had been in her present position. "Nine years," she replied. And what was the average length of time anyone had been in her department? "Two." 'Nuff said. Stabilizers tend to stay in jobs, relationships, and projects longer than is productive for them. For them, too much rushing results in pressure, but too much delay, in frustration.

If you are a Stabilizer, you have an even temperament, put people at ease, and make the work atmosphere relaxed by reducing conflict. You are a true bridge over troubled waters. In fact, your niceness often gets you into trouble. Often, like the girl in *Oklahoma!*, you can't say no, thereby heaping upon yourself more work than you can manage. You put the needs of others first, and the resentment you feel gets suppressed rather than expressed. I often recommend assertiveness training for Stabilizers.

You function very well with procedures and routine. You probably have a work space with plants and pictures of your loved ones. You take in information and are supportive and dependable while radiating calm. In bridge, you bid in a traditional fashion and rarely take chances.

You like environments and processes that are traditional. You question why things should be changed just for change's sake. If a long-standing procedure changes, you are inclined to say, "Couldn't we talk about this first?" Stabilizers want things to be permanent. That is why security is a top priority for them.

You Stabilizers must have missions which concern preservation, community service, continuity, nurturing, and permanence. You must keep the world in balance and stable. You are the glue which holds things together.

Friendly Advice for Stabilizers:

1) take the initiative
2) say no more often
3) work on flexibility and spontaneity
4) learn to face conflict and give criticism

Analyzers

Analyzers contribute a detailed, careful approach to life which enables them to deliver quality. They are the watchdogs for doing things right according to rules and regulations, collecting and analyzing data to insure accuracy and precision.

Would YOU want your surgeon to be a Doer? "Let's get this operation over, I've got my golf game this afternoon and I have to beat Dr. Soandso. What? I accidentally took out the patient's appendix instead of the gall bladder? Oh well, the patient is better off without it." If you need an operation, you'll want your surgeon to be an Analyzer!

Analyzer Trish came to her first Life Mission session armed with twelve different neatly-stacked career tests in alphabetical order. She hadn't yet made up her mind about the results because she needed a little more information. I knew right away she was an Analyzer because they are the information addicts, preferring thorough, copious detail and careful analysis to get results.

If Analyzer is your PM, you like things to be rational and organized. Talking is not your favorite way of communicating. You are far more likely to use non-verbal methods more effectively.

You make decisions with difficulty because you must weigh all the evidence. You have your information ready, your credentials in order, and your facts straight. You prepare a lot of questions which serve to clarify any fuzzy issue. You are not apt to let something slip through your fingers without careful scrutiny! Since you are sensitive about how things ought to be done, it may take you longer to decide what you want, but your choices are always well-informed.

You expect punctuality, organization, and detailed agenda rather than the slapdash approach of the Doers. Chaos can get in the way of your need for clarity. You work in a neat, focused, and serious manner, and could easily find last year's memo to the neighbors about mowing too early in the morning. You often confuse process with solutions and delay making decisions because you have too much information. Watch that you avoid analysis paralysis with too much data.

You're the bridge player who knows the most obscure conventions and plays according to Hoyle. You know all the rules by heart, and you play by them. You fare best in an atmosphere of deliberation and weighing the evidence. You will not want to go with risky ventures but rather opt for the safe bet. Environments which suit you well are ones in which there are clear definitions of what is expected and slow, patient, accurate, investigative approaches are needed. You are a quality control person. Look at Laurie:

Leery Laurie

A quiet, deliberate woman with carefully coiffed hair and a penetrating look, Laurie came up with a creative

41

new type of business venture involving office design. Laurie was leery of making the transition to self-employment. (Going into business for themselves can often be difficult for Analyzers.) Laurie had made the transition only after preparing a two-year business plan, thoroughly researching her market, seeing a marketing consultant, and taking several tests.

She was very aware of her strong points (planning, design, calculating). They enabled her to overcome a lot of personal resistance to going solo, and the courage to work on her lesser strengths of assertiveness and initiation. She has gotten closer to her mission, which is to enhance environments, particularly interior ones.

If you are an Analyzer, your mission must incorporate safety, protection, accuracy, quality, or research and development. You complete with precision what the Doers have initiated. Your mission must deal with preserving quality, especially that which is crucial to human survival. Your contribution is of life and death importance to us all.

Friendly Advice for Analyzers:

1) learn to make decisions faster and stick with them
2) learn when to stop gathering information
3) avoid a rigid approach to life
4) be willing to take more risks

Your PM is the way you express yourself most authentically. It reflects your creative process and mission. Understanding your PM not only gives life shape and direction, but also a framework within which to carry out your mission *in the manner most characteristic of you.* Armed with self-awareness, you can develop options and crystallize them into your quest.

Mission seekers do it *à la mode!*

Chapter Three

The Creative Connection

A cat said to a squirrel: "How wonderful it is that you can so uner-
ringly locate buried nuts, to nurture you through the winter!" The
squirrel said: "To a squirrel, what would be remarkable, would be a
squirrel who was unable to do such things!"

*I*t's a myth that creativity is an elusive quality only
some people are born with. As our squirrel would
say, "Nuts!" If you feel that you must sculpt like Michelangelo, write poetry like Emily Dickinson, or com-
pose like Beethoven in order to be creative, wait a
minute! Could Emily Dickinson paint, Michelangelo
sing, Marie Curie write poetry, or Ludwig van Beethoven understand bacteria? Probably not! And it
doesn't matter. What matters is that they nurtured *their*
own creativity.

Everyone has the ability to be creative. You have it,
I have it. The important thing is that you tap your inner
Source and express *your* creative capacities, whatever
they may be. In an article titled "Creativity in Self-
Actualizing People," psychologist Abraham Maslow

43

said, "I learned . . . that a first-rate soup is more creative than a second-rate painting and that, generally, cooking or parenthood or making a home could be creative while poetry need not be; it could be uncreative."

The purpose of this chapter is 1) to help you recognize, appreciate, and develop your creativity, 2) relate the creative process to your PM and, 3) put that creativity in the service of your Life Mission. Strengthening the connection to your creativity will increase your self-esteem, as well as affirm and enrich the inventive storehouse within you. Work on the chapter's techniques daily and the results will truly amaze you.

Creativity and Life Mission

Creativity is the link for accessing your Life Mission. Paul Torrance has defined creativity as ". . . the process of becoming sensitive to problems, deficiencies, gaps in knowledge, missing elements, disharmonies . . . identifying the difficulty; searching for solutions . . ." In other words, you will be better able to deal with your problems and design your life as you want it to be if you develop your creativity.

Creativity connects you with your innermost self, from which all your answers come. Creativity is a non-linear, non-logical method of gaining information. No amount of list making, skill identification, vocational tests, or reason can really explain the passion for a mission like, say, making soap (such as Dr. Bronner writes about on his soap labels).

We'll look now at what creativity is, why it's important, and how to transform stumbling blocks into building blocks for your mission.

44

Creativity: A Class Act

Creativity is fundamental to the human condition, to personal growth and of course most importantly, to your Life Mission. The absence of creativity contributes to unhappiness, dissatisfaction, and lack of productivity. Wherever innovation and exploration are discouraged, jobs become routine and boring. People then become frustrated because they are blocked from self-expression.

At the beginning of the semester, I asked the members of a class called *Women and the Creative Process* if they thought they were creative. Many doubted that they were. I asked students to bring something imaginative they had done to the last class session and share it with others. Fourteen weeks later, they brought an amazing variety of creations to that last class.

One woman read poetry about her grandmother, material she had never showed to anyone. Another brought in mobiles. A third wrote some Haiku poetry in Japanese and she was an American! One woman brought in house plans she had designed and kept secret from her family for years. Everyone had done something she was proud of. There were lots of laughs and tears that evening as the women expressed themselves openly, many for the first time.

Animals, too, demonstrate the importance of creativity. A TV program showed a baboon sitting listlessly in a cage. Then someone gave it computer paper to play with. The next scene showed the animal racing around the cage happily tossing the pages in the air, sliding on them, and having a wonderful time. The baboon had something to stimulate its brain.

And then there was the experiment with baby rats. Every day researchers would come to the cages and

45

give baby rats new toys. They responded positively to the stimulation and variety their toys provided and literally began lining up in front of the cages to wait for their daily "fix."

Broken Connections

When your life is stimulating and full of variety, you'll react joyfully like those baboons or baby rats. But without tools for the imagination, people listlessly go through the motions of life. They have broken the connection to their creative selves. It's a common phenomenon in the late twentieth century—why?

Research suggests that much of our creativity is suppressed as early as age seven. In the 1970's, many classes in the arts were passed over in favor of "practical" subjects such as business, science, or technical areas. The ability to get a job, to earn money, and to get ahead became more important. What was the value of learning to play the piano? To draw? To write a poem? To understand Greek mythology? To understand the lessons of history? That won't buy a condo or a BMW.

If your school was like mine, you were rewarded more for regurgitating facts than for what you could dream or shape with your mind. You were encouraged to get 100 on your tests rather than inspired to use your imagination. The message was clear: creativity is a frill, icing on the cake, or something to use in your spare time—or for loony artists.

Add to this the effect of the tube. Before the average person reaches the age of twenty-one, they will have spent a total of five years watching television. Although some educational and public television programs are excellent, chances are these are not the programs people watch. Constant input from TV, radio, and movies, etc., leaves no time for inner reflection and sorting things out. Imagine what growth and insight a person could gain if a total of five years were spent in cultivating their creativity!

There are three major factors contributing to the decline of creativity.

1. "I Think, Therefore I Am"

Creativity depends on a person's willingness to keep their mind alert, open, fertile, curious, and above all to use that mind to think. But basic thinking skills have declined. In a recent study on school children, it was found that they could easily solve problems with a calculator. When asked how many people could fit into a bus under certain conditions, children would give answers like 36.7, indicating they had failed to consider whether their answer made sense. (Would you like to be in a bus with 36.7 people?)

Technology has given people the false notion that they can abdicate their responsibility to think. Recently I stood at a cash register watching the clerk struggle to add up my purchases. Finally, he turned to his calculator and exclaimed: "Thank God the machines have to think and we don't!" To be sure, machines can retrieve information, calculate, and relieve much of the need for remembering things, but they do not replace the need for personal inner processing of information. When Einstein was asked his telephone number, he said he didn't remember and didn't need to clutter up his brain with such information. For that he could use a telephone book. He wanted to use his brain for thinking. Technology in the hands of unthinking people is unthinkable (no pun intended). In fact, because you can use computers for storing information instead of your head, it leaves lots more room to use your imagination and far fewer excuses for not using it.

2. Ignorance Is Not Bliss

Ignorance is bliss, the saying goes. (Well if that's true, why aren't more people happy?) Technology gives power to a degree never possible in history. But power without the ability to think creatively is a deadly combination. Take the individuals in a missile site somewhere under the earth. Without the ability to think they could wipe everyone off the map with one press of a button.

Information on just about anything is available. It's not possible to stick your head in the sand and say "I don't know" or "I don't have to think." Ignorance is a cop-out. You understand the effects of alcohol on your body, what cigarettes will do to your lungs, and what will happen if you choose to lie out in the sun too much. And, if you are doing drugs, you are aware (even if you don't care) that you are destroying the capacities of your brain.

Instant access to other countries through information and travel have removed any last vestiges of global ignorance through isolation. The world is a single connected unit, no longer consisting of separate countries with strange and quaint ways of doing things. Contaminated air in one part of the world will drift into another, just as the radiation of Chernobyl polluted the West. Likewise, ignorance in one country affects another. Burying your head in the sand won't do any longer. You have a mandate to be alert, aware, creative, and wise.

3. The Future Isn't What It Used to Be

You won't solve tomorrow's problems with yesterday's methods. Life choices used to involve survival issues such as staying alive, getting crops to grow, keeping warm, or managing with a third unwanted pregnancy.

It used to be that you would pursue the same career as your father or mother. A parent's career choices automatically became yours. No longer. Farmer? Druggist? Minister? Shoemaker? Even if you carry on the family tradition, you probably won't do it for life.

To make matters more difficult, career choices themselves are more complex than at any time on the planet. There are likely to be, on the average, from three to five career changes in a lifetime in addition to several lateral shifts (i.e., staying in the same kind of job, but moving to another company). Whew!

You can't manage these rapid changes without imaginative thinking. Today questions of a moral, ethical, and personal nature such as "Who am I?", "How can I maximize my potential?", "What is my Life Mission?", unlike earlier survival questions, must be answered with the intuitive (right) side of the brain, which sees and processes things in a holistic manner. The foundation for supporting these changes is a solid mission.

Blocks and Creativity

"Sure, I'd love to be creative, but I find myself totally blocked!" an exasperated client said to me recently. If you are blocked, too, and are eager to "get on with it," this next section is for you especially. You can turn those stumbling blocks into building blocks. How?

Treat blocks as friendly signs for attention! They may be an indicator of something you want because they

49

have to do with things you like. Look at a statement such as "I'm blocked from doing the wash, paying the bills, or defleaing the cat!" Using the word 'blocked' in this context is absurd. A block means a chronic inability to perform a mental or creative function. Thus if you are blocked from a mission, from writing a story, or from solving a problem, it means you are separated from something creative and challenging. It means the creative energy flow is stopped.

You get rid of blocks by redirecting your energy. Start swimming downstream and go with your creative flow!

Exercise 3.1: FOUR STEPS TO TRANSFORM BLOCKS

Be the kid on the block instead of having blocks on the kid. Transform those stumbling blocks into building blocks! You need to understand your block, first, before you can transform it or move beyond it. In following exercise we'll show you how to:

1. examine the form.
2. identify the connection between you and the block (the reason for creating it).
3. transform it.
4. find the meaning you see in your block.

First, give definite shape to your block until you can identify its form. If it helps, recall the situation which has caused the block and feel how it is affecting you physically. Figuring the connection between the form and the nature of your block will clarify your own role in the process. You created that particular block. What is it telling you about yourself?

Remember, if you can create it, you can transform it. Every person's block is quite individual in appearance. Work on the most effective way of transforming the shape of your block. We'll look at three cases—one in greater detail—of ways people have mastered their blocks. Let's look at Jane, Irene, and John.

Jane's Blob

She thought of her block as filled with some sort of slippery substance, elusive, heavy, black, and massive. When she tried to do anything with it, it would slide around, and she couldn't hold it. Unable to get rid of this blob, Jane squirmed in her seat just talking about it. In her case, shrinking or demolishing it wouldn't have been the right way to tackle her slimy blob. She literally never got a handle on things because she couldn't focus on them.

Jane had never had to make choices. At 38, she had not even signed a check for herself. Her husband decided everything. When they went out to eat, she'd habitually say, "Whatever you want." Jane rarely had an independent opinion. She got in touch with her unwillingness to commit to anything and her dependency on keeping things slippery. Jane transformed her blob into a white laser beam which directed a current of energy towards the matter she was refusing to deal with. Whenever Jane created new blobs (when she tried to avoid focusing), she redirected them into that beam and focused on her issue.

Irene's Chasm

On the other hand, Irene, a legal secretary, had been putting off a turn in her career for eight years. Her block was a huge chasm. It was so deep and threatening that she had no way of getting across. She was stalled at the edge. She had always stopped short of following her inclination to become a lawyer and had created a huge chasm between herself and her goal.

She constructed fanciful ways to bridge it, taking cues from her imagination (and a vast storehouse of reading). She designed a delightful companion, Old Mother West Wind, who helped blow her over the chasm whenever it appeared. OMWW would simply furrow her brow, take a huge breath, and lift Irene gently over the gap with ease. Irene was comforted by the image of OMWW lending her help.

Actually OMWW was the nurturing force within Irene that she was reluctant to use. Her block resulted from a feeling that she had to do everything herself. She had created the block because of her feelings of isolation. She began to see there were forces outside of herself which could help her if she first accepted responsibility for her actions.

Now we'll look at John's case, going through all four steps of the process:

John's Journey

1. Describing the Block: Getting To Know You. John had a block that looked like a huge concrete wall. There was no way to jump over, go under, or penetrate it. It was unlike anything he had ever seen in reality. Even the Empire State Building paled in comparison. He was both afraid of and intimidated by his block.

2. Connection: Identify Why You Created the Block. A frail man with intense eyes and a wan smile, John had reluctantly followed his father's footsteps in a retail store in a Western city. He realized why he had made the wall so imposing. Since he felt he could not be strong and big, he created something he'd never be able to get over, so he thought. Getting in touch with his feelings of powerlessness and worthlessness, John felt too puny to climb over that big wall. When he talked about it, he would actually shrink back in the chair and close off his body.

3. Method: Transform the Block. First John stood up and imagined that he was Superman, endowed with superior powers to change anything. Then he actually visited a construction site where a crew was demolishing an old office building. Finally, he imagined himself demolishing buildings. Skyscrapers disappeared before his very eyes. Then he practiced doing the same thing to his own block, the wall. While demolishing it, John practiced transforming the wall's energy, feeling it course through his body where he felt weakest, in his chest, arms and hands.

4. Meaning: Relate the Block to Your Career. (It was a revelation for John to see himself as strong and powerful as Superman. During his entire career he had been holding himself back in weak and insignificant positions. Whenever thoughts of helplessness in his career emerged, John practiced this demolition method. Slowly, John began to transform this wall into his mission because he now knew that he was his own source of strength. As long as you have creativity, blocks will be present. It's part of the process. The good news is each time one appears and you deal with it, the transformation gets easier. Then you can move through the block and beyond.)

On Your Path

You can also use guided imagery to further help you transform your block. Record the following suggestions onto a tape for yourself or have someone read them to you slowly.

Prepare for this guided tour of the mind by sitting in a relaxed position with legs uncrossed. Take a deep breath and let it out slowly. Close your eyes, and allow the images in your mind's eye to follow whatever the voice tells you. Don't feel obligated to create everything slavishly. Simply go with what comes to you. (If you have problems visualizing, consult Chapter 10.)

Imagine that you are taking a walk on a beautiful summer day. You're in the country, heading down a path. Pay attention to the smells, sights, and sounds around you. PAUSE. As you approach a fork in the road, you notice two signs—one pointing to the right and one to the left. Make note of what you see on the signs and pick one fork to continue on.

As you proceed, you come to a barrier. Stop, take a close look at this barrier and pass by it with the greatest of ease. PAUSE.

In the distance you see a house. Look at the house carefully, observing its style and size. No one is home, yet it feels like you are expected and that you should go in. The door is open, and you go in, moving from room to room, savoring all the things you see. Observe the furniture, the windows, the decor of this house. PAUSE. Now go up the stairs to the second floor where there is a long hallway with light shining from a room.

You head down the hall towards this room, and upon entering, you see a young child playing quietly amidst toys and other objects. You join the child in play awhile. PAUSE. After awhile, the child selects one of

54

the toys, and hands it to you, saying, "This is a gift to you from me." You thank the child and leave the room quietly, treasuring your object as you return downstairs. Go out the front door with your object and resume your walk. Return with your object to the space you are in.

Use the following questions as discussion guides with a friend or counselor, since many of the insights become clearer with dialogue. Put the answers in your notebook for reference.

1. What were you wearing and how did you feel during your walk?
2. What did the path and surroundings look like?
3. What path did you take at the fork? What was written on the signs?
4. Describe the path after the fork.
5. What did the barrier look like? The barrier is akin to the block you put in your path. Did you have any trouble getting by it? How did it feel when you did? How did you transform it?
6. Describe the house itself. What kind of house did you choose? Cottage? Lodge? Rustic? Colonial? Castle? The house is often a symbol of the self. It reflects much of what you see in yourself. Did you feel you could move around with ease? Was it open and inviting or dark and closed?
7. Describe the interior of the house. Was it big, small, bright, airy, dark, full of objects, deserted? Were there lots of windows or few?
8. Describe the experience with the child in the room. What did the child look like? What was the child playing when you entered the room? What kind of playing did you do with the child? Did s(he) have any difficulty in selecting an object for you? What object did the child give you and how did it affect you? Were you surprised

to receive it? Did you feel okay about taking it with you and keeping it? How did this object affect you emotionally? What does it mean to you?

Play and Your Creative Child Within

Play is absolutely essential because it helps remove blocks and release creativity. But play is often associated with children. Being the child is a marvelous way to enjoy, fantasize, and laugh. The adult world rarely encourages play. Often, adults permit themselves to play only in the context of sports. How long has it been since you have allowed yourself to be a child again? To be silly, clown at work, or play children's games?

In a corporate workshop, I played a music cassette and asked the participants to doodle, finger paint, or draw whatever they pleased while listening to the music. Soon they began to have fun right within those company walls! When we discussed the exercise later, participants said they had gotten in touch with grade school experiences and sensorial memories (smells, sights, sounds) from that time. While finger painting, one participant exclaimed, "I haven't allowed myself to do this in years. I feel like I'm back in Third Grade!"

Creative children frequently daydream, fidget or are impatient in school. They are likely to hear "Toe the line! Be like the others! Memorize the facts to get good grades! Pay attention to the teacher! Don't daydream!" It's little wonder that our inner creative child is so elusive. It takes courage to reconnect to her/him.

Dana told me a personal story which matched almost exactly an example I had been using in workshops for two years!

"When I was in the third grade, we were asked to draw trees in art class. The teacher hadn't told us what the tree was to look like, but when she came around to my desk, she frowned and said: "THAT'S not the way a tree is supposed to look. Draw it this way." She drew the kind of tree you see in children's books. It didn't match my version. That moment froze vividly in my memory, and from then on, I never dared to be creative. I just did what I was told." Suddenly, Dana had parted with her creative self and learned the "accepted" way of doing things.

Dana was truly blocked from finding creative solutions to her career needs by a "minor" incident in her childhood. If you're having trouble with blocks, access your inner child by going to a playground, visiting a children's theater, making something a child would or just plain PLAY awhile (no fair taking a child along—just go by yourself).

Your answers in this visualization have a lot to do with how you envision your path, what your barriers look like, and what you might give yourself for a gift. Your path is also a way of looking at your mission. The word career means "vehicle," from the Middle Latin word *carraria* (from which our words *car* or *carriage* are derived). You can think of career as the vehicle you use to travel your path of life.

Jealousy and Envy: Two Friendly Blocks

Certain kinds of blocks can be friendly clues about what you are neglecting. Remember when you were really jealous about something? If you're like me, you tried to tell yourself it wasn't "right," but you had those feelings anyway. Well, here's a way to make jealousy work for you.

When Gloria Steinem came to L.A. to promote her latest book, I saw the announcement in the paper, and felt jealous. Now I ask you, would I get envious about a famous stock market analyst autographing a book? No way! But being green with envy over Gloria Steinem meant I needed to be writing and promoting a book, and that part of my mission is to be a respected female thinker and communicator.

I was blocked in several areas and used my jealousies to help determine which one to work on first. (If prioritizing is one of your blocks, you'll profit doubly with this example.) List the person who triggered your jealousy and the circumstances in which the jealousy was aroused. Here's my example:

Person Involved	*Circumstance of Trigger*	*Lesson to Be Learned*
a) Steinem	booksigning parties	need to start novel, need to buy computer
b) Rodgers and Hammerstein	feature story on their careers on TV	take songwriting course, start composing
c) music prof	seeing all his electronic music equipment	read about electronic music, buy a synthesizer, increase income
d) a friend	visiting high tech office	need to be better organized, upgrade office equipment

Which is your greatest jealousy, and what do you need to get going on? Compare each set of letters (for example, "a" to "b") and pick one from each pair. Add up the totals for each of the letters selected. In the example below, my highest score was *a*, which shows that I was most envious of Steinem, and that the book was the most important thing for me to be working on. (Surprise!)

a *vs* b ___a___   a *vs* d ___a___   b *vs* d ___b___

a *vs* c ___a___   b *vs* c ___c___   c *vs* d ___c___

Score: a __3__   b __1__   c __2__   d __0__

You can use this method for any kind of prioritizing. Restrict yourself to a maximum of 10 items or less (or you'll be spending nights wading through your list instead of working on the winner). Begin with your greatest block, and chip away at others over time.

Nine Building Blocks to a Creative Life Mission

The following are nine ideas about creativity which you can apply to your mission search.

1. Creativity is novelty. You bring something into being which did not exist in that form before. The important thing is that it is new for you. But there is a difference between repeating what someone else has already created (reinventing the wheel) and doing something new and insightful. If 487 other people have already discovered what you did, it makes your effort no less creative. What counts is the intention. You wanted to explore rather than recreate.

The distinction is important. Many people feel

59

everything has already been done, so why bother—that wouldn't be creative. But why does the tenth recording of Beethoven's Fifth Symphony, old song favorites, or another French cookbook get released? Because there are always new ways of looking at everything. Creativity is personal expression. There are no rules of right and wrong. It's important to explore, investigate, risk, and look at things in new ways—like writing a novel in verse form.

Likewise, your mission is unique, singular, and without parallel to anyone else's because it's coming from you (unless you have a clone somewhere). So don't say its been done before. The world needs your version!

2. Creativity is upsetting the status quo. Challenge how things are done, turn things around, upside down or inside out. There are aspects to creativity which have their painful side. When you create something, you are ending, possibly destroying, something else. Galileo showed that the earth was no longer the center of the universe, making people recognize their dependency on the sun and challenging theological teachings. That was upsetting, but it was part of his mission of scientific exploration and finding the truth.

Your mission, too, is going to upset the apple cart in some way. Or do you not want your pebble to make waves?

3. Creativity is taking risks. Risks are like spreading clandestine leaflets, such as the White Rose group did in Nazi Germany, painting a face green instead of flesh colored, coining a new word, making people laugh when they are ill or refusing to go along with the way everybody else does. It's doing something you've never done before without knowing the outcome.

Creative risks can cause rifts, enlighten, rattle at the cages of the mind, infuriate, or elevate. Keep in mind that your mission might cause trouble among your friends. The greatest risk of all, making changes in yourself, can be threatening to your loved ones, because you are breaking the rules they are used to.

4. Creativity is making new connections. Some of the most common inventions happened because somebody combined two things or ideas together. Men's jockey shorts, for instance, were a direct result of connecting their design to that of baby diapers. What do you get when you link cars and hotels? Motels! The list is endless. You'll find that the things you love can be connected together in new ways (commonly called a mission). Combine politics, fitness, and acting, for example, and you get the main ingredients of Jane Fonda's mission.

5. Creativity is following through on your curiosity. You may wonder about something, ask a "what if" question and leave it at that or you may decide to go farther. Someone might say "I had that idea way back in 1965." Sure, it was there, but what happened after that? Creativity without follow-through is like leaving flour on the shelf forever. It's of little good unless it's used. When you were a child, you dreamed, perhaps about being a princess, a knight, a fire fighter, or a clown. You gave yourselves permission to let go. As adults you have the luxury of fantasizing and fulfilling the dream. A dancer once commented that all the other kids dreamt of being a dancer, and she became one. She wanted to know more about it. Explore your curiosity!

61

6. Creativity is being different. Conditioning might be okay for your hair—it keeps everything in its place—but it's not healthy for creativity. Being creative means moving outside the pack, altering the rules, and thinking independently. In a *Los Angeles Times* interview Jacques Cousteau said, "I don't look at other people's films. I don't have time. I'm not interested in what other people are doing, because we are doing it differently . . . A movie maker has his own personality and sees things differently . . . I make my films to be different. It will be my way of looking at things. I am convinced that [a] world where people enjoy themselves the proper way—in creation, creating anything—and thinking only about the creation they are doing is a better world than a world in which people preach . . ."

Unless you want to live a carbon copy life, get used to being different. You mission can only be different if you are.

7. Creativity is surrender to process. The most important factor is the path which leads to a goal. The steps to this book began with the design of creativity seminars. Eventually, that led to a bookmark and the bookmark has turned into the chapters of this book. It was a process which my Source already knew way back in 1982! I simply surrendered to it. Creativity means process before product, not a popular notion today. You must let your mission be/come all it needs to without constant control and squelching.

8. Creativity is sharing your gifts. Emily Dickinson put her poems in a drawer. Leonardo da Vinci carried the Mona Lisa around with him for 20 years, constantly making changes and "improvements."

Sometimes people are unwilling to give of their creativity to certain groups. Bach never shared his musical teachings with his daughters. Artur Rubenstein was unwilling to perform in Germany, and Thomas Mann couldn't return to live there anymore. But when Russian émigré Vladimir Horowitz journeyed back to Moscow for an emotional homecoming, there were tears of relief and joy from his sharing.

Let go of your gift and release it for the world to have. A part of you goes with it but never gets lost. To be creative, you must surrender yourself to the process of giving and receiving. There is no ownership here. You are simply a divine conduit through which all creative juices flow.

Some people have no problems with creating, but must deal with the separation of their creation from themselves. A story by E. T. A. Hoffmann called "The Golden Pot," which takes place in Paris at the time of Louis the Fourteenth, illustrates a creator's inability to separate from his creation.

An eccentric, but highly talented goldsmith makes the most fabulous jewelry in all of Paris. Over a period of time a series of murders of aristocratic women occurs, and no one can figure out who the murderer is. A lengthy investigation reveals that all the victims had commissioned jewelry from a certain goldsmith. The artist, as it turns out, had an uncontrollable need to kill his victims because he was unable to part with any of his creations. The story shows that it is imperative to release addictive attachment to one's creations.

Your mission is a gift, and a gift by definition is both received and given. You can't have one without the other. If you block either direction, you will deny the world or yourself the joy of your contribution.

9. Creativity is accepting yourself. To resist BEING WHO YOU ARE is the greatest hindrance to your creativity. The more you resist, the greater the pain, and it impedes expression by stifling the self. It's a constant paradox: whatever happens needs to, yet you must do the work necessary for it to take place. You are both creator/created, potter/pot, sender/receiver. Seeing a mission as surrender and as a calling places you in the position of hearing your inner voice and responding to it. To be on the wrong path is to turn a deaf ear to yourself.

Creativity requires you to give up old patterns to which you have become accustomed. It requires abandonment to yourself as source and resource, beginning and end. Creativity shows you the way to your mission. The mission in turn expresses your true essence.

The subsequent chapters forming the acronym CREATIVITY represent a different turn of the kaleidoscope to see your individual Life Mission pattern. They will help you get in tune with your Source and maximize your potential.

It's time now to unleash the self that has been awaiting your call. Creative expression is shared self-love in action. Connect with the talent which is most divinely yours. All aboard!

Part Two

CREATIVE PATHS TO YOUR LIFE MISSION

Chapter Four

Clear Your Mind

I magine an attic filled with old albums and letters, trunks with clothes never again to be worn, discarded furniture and tons of cobwebs. In the same way as that attic, your brain is often filled to the top with chatter, criticism, old business, anxious thoughts, and incessant dialogue. It needs, as Norman Cousins phrased it, "the blessing of silence."

You can think three times as fast as you talk or listen. Your mind races constantly. Try this: look up from this page and time yourself. For one minute, try to think of nothing. When you are done, estimate how many thoughts you had. If you had none, skip this chapter and go on.

For most people, the mind conjures up thousands of thoughts a day. Here's how the opening paragraph might actually sound in your mind when you read it or someone reads it to you.

Imagine an attic, *I don't have an attic, I live in a condo,* filled with old albums and letters, *Did I remember to leave a note for Madge to mail those letters?* trunks with clothes never again to be worn, *Isn't that a quaint way of putting it? she's really cute sometimes,* discarded furniture and tons of cobwebs, *I bet Harry will never get around to cleaning out his car.*

The italicized sentences show examples of an intruding mind. You can't get much done in this muddled state.

Let Me Make This Perfectly Clear

The word clear actually means both *clear in sound,* and to *cry out.* You must have a clear mental space to promote sound thinking. You can't think in a mental room crammed to the ceiling. Clean out your attic so that brain of yours has an uncluttered room. By weeding and sorting out the clutter from your mind, you can get organized, focus on your goals, and make connections. Your mission is crying out to be heard.

Give It Room!

In this chapter you will learn how to 1) reduce outside interference, 2) cut down on the garbage you feed your mind, and 3) use a seven-step program which I call CYM (Clear Your Mind) to rest and recharge your brain on a daily basis. The objective is to keep your mind open and free of obstruction so you can zero in on your mission.

Here's a quick checklist to tell if your mind is clear:

- Do *The Who* suggest hardness of hearing or a rock group?
- Do you usually play the radio when you drive?
- Do you have the TV on when you converse?
- Do you avoid periods of silence (30 minutes or longer)?
- Do you usually notice music in stores?
- Do you jog with a Walkman? (Or walk with a tape running?)
- Do you play background music in your home?
- Do you like to do several things at once (eat and read, watch TV, and write letters)?
- Do you find it difficult to go several minutes without thinking a thought?
- Do you watch more than two hours of TV a day (three hours if it's PBS)?
- Do you avoid quiet places, like libraries?
- Do you take a radio or TV on vacation?
- Do you eat in restaurants even with loud music playing?
- Do you answer the phone even during times when you are concentrating on something?
- Do you talk only when you need to?
- Do you constantly rehash the past or anticipate the future in your thoughts?

If you answered even half of the above with "yes" or "I don't know," your mind is crammed. You need to get rid of mental litter, admit only the information which you really can use, and ignore the rest. The most popular part of the TV program "CBS Sunday Morning" is the 2–3 minute end segment showing beautiful and peaceful scenes from nature without comment. At a local health club, the executive locker room is quiet. It has none of the junk music piped in to the regular locker area. At heart, most people know the value of silence and serenity.

Minding Your Brain

Your brain is a storehouse of information, a place for memories, and a think tank. It would take four minutes to write a number equal to all the neutrinos (the smallest particle in the universe). But you'd need ninety years at the same pace to write the number of synapses (210 billionth power) in the human brain.

The brain comprises only about two and a half to three percent of the body weight, but it takes about twenty-two percent of the body's energy to fuel it. If you took out your brain and spread it out on the floor, you'd have a circumference of over two and one half feet (and an unwrinkled brain). That organ upstairs is built for action and power, but you must take care of it before it can perform well.

A well-tuned brain enables you to make choices, take chances, be creative, and above all to think. The world needs your intelligence operating at full strength, and you need that intelligence to realize your Life Mission.

Cogito, Ergo Sum: I *Think, Therefore I Am*

Thinking is an underdeveloped skill. You probably didn't learn it in school. But the inability to think is pervasive. Ask the phone company about its rate structure, a company about its mission, listen to a TV talk show, or a presidential press conference. If you're lucky, you'll get coherent statements fifty percent of the time.

Companies would ask me what benefits the participant could expect from creativity workshops. I said: "The ability to think." They responded by saying, "Well, when we have time, we'll give it some consideration. But first we need to tackle more important issues. We'll look into it when all our basic (!) training

70

courses are completed." No amount of training will help if the trainee has had a brain bypass. The nice thing about remaining ignorant is that you never suffer from loneliness.

Body vs. Mind

People spend hours working on their bodies, but rarely do they have a program specifically for their minds. They spend more time sorting out their laundry than their thoughts. It's indicative of present culture that there are few workout programs for stretching the imagination, exercising the brain, and lifting the spirits. The late-twentieth-century version of the song *Body and Soul* would be: "I'm all for you body and . . . body."

High school SAT scores have consistently gone down over the years, creativity scores are lower than before, and illiteracy is on the rise. The brain drain, folks, is going on right before (or rather behind) our eyes.

I Feel, Therefore I Know

A disastrous effect of a cluttered brain is that feelings get blocked from giving valuable information. Like cream, they will rise to the top but only when you stop the interference and listen to yourself. Take the example of Claudia:

"I Didn't Know I Felt That"

Claudia was a 44-year-old ranchwoman. She had acted in a couple of high school plays, but after graduating, she had gone on to "better and more serious" things. She reasoned that it was "just a phase everybody went

71

through in school." (Claudia invoked the word "everybody" at precisely the moment she rationalized her choice.)

Never mind that she had taken English literature courses, especially Shakespeare, in college. Never mind that after moving to a small California town, Claudia would drive two hours to Los Angeles to see a new play in town. Since college, Claudia had married, raised four children, volunteered for numerous organizations, including a project for a local amateur theater group, and raised funds for the new high school (making sure they had a good theater in it).

She forgot her love for the theater, she realized, by overloading her brain with things to think and do. As supermom, she had little time to connect to dormant dreams. Claudia never took the time to reflect on the way her life was going, even though the pain of a missed calling took the forms of headaches, angry outbursts, and arguments. Claudia always ended up having "better things to do" than her mission.

I encouraged her to practice Clear Your Mind (CYM) by taking walks and reflecting and by sitting quietly at night listening to her inner voice. No kids, no television, no activities, just Claudia with Claudia. The message was unmistakable: to "do something for herself away from the kids." She visited New York, saw her former high school acting teacher in a play and was reminded of his encouraging words many years back: "If you don't choose it, you'll lose it." Claudia knew it was now or never.

She decided to resume acting and move the family closer to Los Angeles. She gave her husband an ultimatum: "Either accept my new direction, or you'll be playing both father and mother to our three children still at home." (Her acting ability came in handy here.) Luckily for Claudia's husband, he decided to go along with her plan. The relationship was actually saved. Now

Claudia is taking drama courses at a local college and preparing for a theater major.

Claudia accessed her true self by removing the barriers which had clouded her thinking and blocked her creativity. Then she could hear and respond to her mission of self-expression through theater.

Many people, like Claudia, are blocked from their mission because their thinking and feelings are cluttered. CYM gets you in touch with that mission by giving you clarity, focus, and purpose. Once you feel your mission, your deepest wishes, desires, and passions will radiate outward again. When you have rekindled the flame, any sadness will diminish.

The Information Age: Garbage In

Now we'll take a closer look at what's causing cluttered, unclear minds, and what you can do to clear your mind. You can't have a mission with a brain in remission. Going into remission, however, is the brain's way of self-protection from the ravages of information.

This is an age governed by information—getting it, giving it, and processing it. Much of the time it is junk, or unsolicited, or both. We humans are bombarded daily with ads, radio, TV, Muzak, car radios, signs, computers, and telephones. Garbage in. We may have conquered space but not our neighbor's air space.

The other day I went to a small café and had to endure a radio talk show as my "entertainment." A Basque outdoor restaurant near here has a TV set in the patio. (Don't leave home without it.) Every department store has its own sound system. Movie houses advertise before the show (remember when that didn't happen?) and main thoroughfares and superhighways are draped with billboards.

It's getting tougher to escape this intrusion. You even get mindless ads over the phone when you're trapped on hold. Or you're subjected to music which I hope you never listen to otherwise. Computers with prerecorded telephone messages intrude upon your life.

Even worse is the juxtaposition of mindless TV ads with serious programming. A visiting professor from France told me he got up to watch TV in the early morning and was delighted to find a lecture on Voltaire. "Suddenly," he said, "this gorilla began to move forward on the screen and I couldn't for the life of me make the connection to Voltaire." Welcome to American commercial breaks. Is it any wonder people have trouble connecting one idea to another?

Instant accessibility has made it almost impossible for people to be unreachable. Even cars and airplanes now have phones. Our society truly suffers from excess access. The only way to guarantee silence is to subpoena government and military officials to testify before a Congressional committee. And then there are the people who like to give you a piece of their mind. They're generous and like to dish up a big piece, too. Friends, relatives and partners can be relentless in their advice and chatter. Sometimes it's easier to turn off a radio than get rid of a meddling significant other.

Decisions, Decisions, Decisions

Because intrusive information is so abundant, your brain is in a constant state of stimulation. Try to make a decision in this overloaded state. It's like thinking in a shop with ten TVs blaring.

Now add to this mess the *types of decisions* you are required to make. Buy anything and you're inundated with choices. Checks with or without address? In color or plain? Lined or with pictures? With carbon or stubs? Designer motifs or a personal message? Beginning with what number?

Or take buying a car. Henry Ford once said, " You can have any color car you want, just so long as it's black." Were it only so now, Henry! Besides the color, you have to choose the model, the style (stick or automatic?), the type of tires, paint (metallic or not?), and what kind of glass (tinted or plain?). The choices go on. Air conditioning? Power steering? Digital radio with or without tape deck? Alarm system? Extended warranty? And then there's the insurance. No wonder buying a car, or anything else for that matter, is so traumatic.

To say it's all hopeless and life is too difficult is not the solution. In spite of today's complexities, if decision making is too much trouble, too difficult, or results in paralysis, you've got a thinking problem. Your brain is no doubt on overload.

To stay clear-headed, you must remove yourself from any outside stimuli which do not contribute to your growth and mission. You are responsible for reducing the outside clutter in your life. How would you react if someone suddenly dumped a sackload of garbage on your lawn or in your living room? Or if someone blew smoke in your face? But you allow intrusions almost daily in the form of blaring radios, TV broadcasts, and traffic.

Here are a dozen guidelines to reduce outside stimulation and give your brain the rest it needs to function at highest capacity:

1. Play radios, TV, stereos, only when you are actually listening to them.
2. Do one thing at a time.
3. Focus entirely on what you are doing. (Also helps you with #2.)
4. Speak only when you have something to say. (Needless talk is like outside clutter.)
5. Avoid noise, distractions, and cluttered environments.
6. Avoid contributing to the noise pollution of others.
7. Commit to 30 minutes of quiet time per day (unless you're a Carmelite monk).
8. Agree on some talk-free time when you are with others.
9. Spend a certain period of time each day alone.
10. Find peaceful places in your environment and visit them regularly.

Sounding Off for Silence

A mission is possible only when you can clearly and quietly reflect on it. You can do something about outside interference yourself. One woman in a nearby community collected signatures against leaf blowers because the noise drives people nuts. Result: leaf blowers were allowed only at certain times of the day.

Let companies know you dislike any music in offices or when you are held hostage on hold. Tell restaurants to turn off the awful stuff they play and notify the police about noisy neighbors. Tell the theater manager the movie is too loud. I hate to think what shape most people's ears are in when they permit that kind of volume.

A couple of years back I sat in a dentist's office

waiting to have a tooth pulled. They were playing rock music, enough to jangle my nerves. In spite of my urgent need to have the tooth extracted, I told the receptionist to turn the noise off or the dentist could forget my appointment.

On the positive side, when someone plays music at a decent level, or provides a quiet environment, tell them you appreciate it. Give supportive feedback for efforts to keep your environment safe and sane.

The point is to take positive action and silence the racket going on around you. Don't sit back and allow yourself to become a garbage dump for noise. Most communities now have noise control departments. Call them! Silence is golden. You deserve it and your brain needs it.

Information Age: Garbage from Within

There may be a lot of noise coming from outside, but you contribute even more noise from *inside you*. It's no wonder you are paralyzed in making simple choices. But here's the opportunity to really begin to do something about this nuisance. The only thing you want to be able to hear loud and clear is the wisdom from within.

Get rid of everything else vying for your attention! Even talking to yourself prevents listening to yourself. Those internal tapes, thoughts about how you are doing, comments on your productivity (often the lack thereof), planning and scheduling, reliving the past, obsessing about other people, rehearsing what to say, fearing the future, contribute little to your peace of mind. No wonder you have trouble thinking! Your brain hasn't been given a chance.

Create a Sanctuary of the Mind

For healthy thinking, design your surroundings to include a quiet space. I call it a sanctuary of the mind. A sanctuary is a haven, a place of safety and refuge. Information overload results when people don't permit themselves the gift of sanctuary. The excuses are varied, but the result is the same: "I don't take time for me because I don't deserve it." "I don't have time to take time." "I'll take time after April 15." And on it goes.

But your mission can only make itself heard in an atmosphere of trust, quiet, and repose. It must have your undivided attention, love, and commitment. Your mission must feel that it can communicate to you safely without inside or outside interference.

Less Is More

The sole (soul!) purpose of your sanctuary is for doing nothing. Caution! You have to actively practice such a delicious notion. The solution to clear thinking lies in doing *less*, not more. But this is exactly what you have had drilled into you since childhood: doing something, ANYTHING, is better than doing nothing.

Doing nothing is either felt to be sinful, lazy, or procrastination. Society encourages action, movement, speed, and results. And although these are good things, it's a mistake to think you've got to be in endless motion to achieve. Take Winnie the Pooh. No program, no agenda, no notches on a stick for him. Pooh just *was*.

La Donna Mobile

At age 51, Donna had given her entire life to an insurance agency. An Analyzer, she spent her entire day making lists, inspecting reports, returning phone calls, and checking data. The times she even took off five minutes from work to relax were almost legendary. No time to think, just do, do, do.

I suggested that she take a couple of weeks off from work. An unthinkable idea! "How would they survive without me?" she complained. After some struggle, she relented and began to make all sorts of plans for her two weeks, but none of which included herself. It was to be a long two weeks.

She returned to work tired, resentful, and angry. She had prepared and revised lists forever, planned to the hilt but never gotten around to giving herself space and quiet. It was difficult for Donna to think clearly. The "time off" period showed that even when she had the time, she was unable to take advantage of it. Donna had to do some serious attitude readjustment. She needed rest, to recharge her mind before going into action, and to spend more time alone in quiet meditation.

She cut down on work, took nothing home, and made her weekends absolutely unstructured. Above all, she was to come first before anything—husband, dog, children, house, or friends. Everyday she created a sanctuary of the mind in a space she carefully appropriated for herself in the den.

Soon Donna began to clean out those mental cobwebs. She could see clearly that the first thing to do was to reassess her frenetic job and continue her program of CYM. Donna's mission began to take shape after her fog lifted: to provide an atmosphere of medical security for people. Six weeks later she was on the road to a new job and a rediscovered mission.

Exercise 4.1: GARBAGE IN(SIDE) OUT!

Here are five guidelines for getting rid of garbage from within. If possible, create a special sanctuary space for yourself and actually go to it. The emphasis is on quiet and refuge.

1. Observe when your mind wanders and why. Find a word to get yourself back on track (like egads! or boo!). Avoid situations that entice you into wandering thoughts.

2. Allow any critical inner voices to speak but do not act on their advice. Just like children who want to get your goat, reacting to the critic will do no good. You have to listen and then politely say, "Have a nice day" and go on with your meditation.

3. Pick a definite time of day to address your worries. Instead of fretting in the middle of the night or during work hours or during your sanctuary time, agree with yourself that you will take all your cares under advisement (say between 3–5 p.m. on Thursdays). You will be amazed at how many of them have disappeared by then.

4. Spend at least 15 minutes a day on a right brain activity. You could draw, play music, write with your non-preferred hand, practice yoga, or do whatever will take you out of the verbal into your non-verbal mode.

5. Identify where your negative thoughts are lodged in your body. When you say, "my boss is a pain in the neck," you've located the body area where your boss or whatever else bothers you. Whenever negative thoughts appear, stop, breathe deeply, and imagine that you are breathing through that area. If your neck is tense, breathe into it until your muscles relax.

Turning On to Tuning Out. But Not Forever!

Any method carried to excess, even CYM, is ineffective. Staring at the wall for two days is not what I'm talking about. CYM is a way station, a clearing of the forest to see your way. It's preparation for action, relaxation, and the means to an end.

While CYM is an important step in the process, it is *not the end point.* But you need this step to root out whatever is blocking you or to revive and energize yourself. Think of CYM as the calm before the storm. We're talking about balance in this chapter. A good recipe is just the right amount of reflection and action. So although we are emphasizing CYM, beware of staying in this comfort zone too long!

Witness Jim: Ohm, Ohm on the Range

A student of metaphysics and yoga, Jim was seduced by extreme calm. He lived in a sort of eternal somnambulance. He made lists, spent time on long walks lost in thought, meditated, chanted, and daydreamed. Now these are all good things. But Jim became obsessed with his praying mantra lifestyle, he was so laid back and "tuned out," that he was unable to translate his preparation into results. Jim was like a person who owned a car but never drove it, or a plane standing on the runway which never took off. All systems were go except the one in him.

Exercise 4.2: *YOU HAVE THE RIGHT TO REMAIN SILENT—YOUR 7 STEP CYM PROGRAM*

After reducing information overload from without and within, take time each day to strengthen and maintain this uncluttered state of mind effectively with this seven-step program:

1. Prepare. Select a time when you can rid your environment of distractions and be silent. Tell those you live with to respect your need for quiet. Children must understand that you frequently need to be alone. You don't have to have moral qualms whether or not to pull plugs. Do it! Unhook the phone or put on the answering machine. Go to the quietest room of the house, allowing from 15 minutes to an hour.

2. Relax. Sit down, get comfortable, and begin by deep breathing and focusing on your breath. Keep your upper torso relaxed and still. Begin the exercise when your breathing is steady and deep. Now imagine you are breathing through your feet, then move slowly up through your body, telling each area to "relax." Continue the exercise, breathing mentally through your ankles, continuing on through your lower leg, knees, thighs, buttocks, pelvis, chest, arms, shoulders, neck, face, forehead, and finally to the crown of your head.

3. Drain. Imagine that all that internal pollution is draining slowly out of you through your limbs. When you have finished, feel a glow of inspiration washing down over your crown and all through your body. All tiredness and tensions flow out through your feet and into the floor. Your mind is now free to focus on a specific concern.

Continue your session, and when a thought occurs to you, gently push it aside, as you might do with tender saplings as you walk along a forest path in the spring. Spend at least ten minutes without thinking about anything (not even this book, which will be hard). Your mind is now free to focus on a specific concern.

4. Meditate Actively. The purpose of active meditation at this point is to center on a concern. Sit in a chair or on the floor with legs uncrossed or lie on the floor. Do not meditate in bed, as you might fall asleep. Practice without listening to music and with your eyes closed.

Imagine the question you want to address now moving forward into your consciousness, unobstructed and uncluttered. Wait quietly for guidance. Listen to what you are telling you and disregard any critical voice. Maybe nothing will come to you just now. That's okay, the more you practice CYM, the more it will come to you. The main thing is to practice this technique regularly. You will be paid back with greater ease in dealing with your mission.

Let's see how John used this active meditation. He asked himself what quality was so much a part of him, that if he lost it he'd be a stranger to himself.

Spiritual Moves

John, a former clergyman, felt his unique quality was compassion. He discovered in meditation that he couldn't bear to see his housekeeper exploited by a car dealer, and although he wasn't a lawyer, he personally handled her case by negotiating with the dealer. John also worked on projects for the poor and the homeless. He was incensed over a professor who refused to allow him to make up a test because a project for the poor had conflicted with the exam date (John needed compassion, too.)

As he thought about the transition from the clergy into the film industry, he wondered if compassion is the quality needed in films. But as he discovered, there was a way to use his compassion and spirituality on a much broader scale in documentaries and educational films. His first documentary was on care for people with AIDS. John's capacity for compassion was the key to the success of that film and a central part of his mission.

What is *your* special quality and where could you begin to use it more effectively in the service of your Life Mission?

You can use this meditation technique with great effectiveness for brief periods of time throughout the day. Let's suppose that you work in a busy office with lots of activity, deadlines, typewriters clacking, and phones ringing. You have just about reached your limit when Mr. Frazzle comes in announcing the latest crisis.

This is precisely the time to take 1–3 minutes for a quick flick, as I call it. You can mentally paint the most beautifully serene spot on earth. We'll call it your secret paradise. Put yourself in it and stay as long as you can. If you have to run out to your car or sit on the toilet or go outside to find a spot to meditate, do so. This will serve as a test whether you can give yourself permission to meditate at a time when (or where) it seems inappropriate. Quick flicks can be just as effective as long sessions. Frequent use of these small chunks of time gives you a shot in the arm for creative action.

5. *Read.* Now for at least five minutes, turn to some inspirational reading for the day. You can simply open a book to a random page and read from there. You will find that something on that page will be information you need that very day. For ideas about what books to read, please check the bibliography.

6. *Affirm.* An affirmation is a short positive sentence in the present tense, first person, and describes a quality you want to develop, or something you want to have manifested.

"I will not be afraid" is an example of how not to write an affirmation. Reword that sentence into something positive: "I practice my courage daily," or "I am courageous." An affirmation for this chapter might be " I think easily and my mind is clear," or "I am a serene person." A thought held in the mind is a thought manifested.

At first you may find it hard to believe what you are saying. Exercise trust in your Source, that part of you which knows and manifests what you desire. Affirmations set things in motion from the moment you speak them. Solidify your session by affirming that the solution you have reached or the advice you have heard is manifesting itself now. What you desire will transpire!

7. *Act.* The goal of steps 1–6 is to recharge and prepare yourself in a positive way for the day, as well as to organize and focus your energy. Now move directly thereafter into something active.

Perhaps you might work on your latest book (like I'm doing at this moment), dream up ideas for a project you're working on, or plan your day. You are most creative at this time. The important thing is ultimately to translate your meditative wisdom into ACTION.

Although there are seven parts to the CYM program, you need not do them all in one sitting. It is better to have a looser format than a compulsive, structured one, because then you can use whatever seems right for the particular day. Having a number of possibilities to choose from also gives variety to your meditation. You can also add your own variations. For instance, you might feel like skipping the hour altogether or going for a walk, that's okay, too. Or you might want to chant, sing a favorite song, or dance to music for a few minutes. Use whatever works, whatever gets you in tune with yourself, activated and positively charged for the day. Soon you will develop your own routine, one that works for you. The main thing is to do your CYM program regularly, and be sure that each session includes some quiet time with *absolutely no agenda.*

As Goethe writes in his poem, *In the Forest:*

I walked in the woods, just for me.
I focused on seeking nothing.

Do CYM "just for you." Make room for yourself and listen to yourself. Armed with the advice you get from within, you can move forward with confidence. That's the subject of the next chapter.

Chapter Five

Risk Daily

*L*ife is a risk. The first steps you took as a child were just that. Did you know what to expect? You could have fallen down and hurt yourself (risk does mean incurring possible injury) but something urged you on and you did it. You wanted to walk and you did. Recover that adventurous child within you to get what you really desire. As Raymond Loewy, the famous designer said, "I sought to surprise. I sought excitement and taking chances. I was all ready to fail in order to achieve something grand."

Take actions toward your mission instead of waiting for something to happen.

Risk and Life Mission

Risk means venturing into unknown and untested arenas, moving out of acceptable patterns, and most important, *achieving your unique mission*. Life Mission is a risk, you ask? How come? Isn't it the very thing that is uniquely mine? Yes, and that's the challenge

Many people are not comfortable doing something just for themselves. They prefer to be like parents who speak up for their child but never express anything on their own behalf. And, the pursuit of your mission may alienate you from those who want to squeeze you into their mold. There is enormous seduction in staying with the messages you get from others.

Finding your Life Mission is an intensely *personal* matter. The risk lies in pursuing an individual assignment no one else can fulfill. You can either decide to go for your calling or not. Avoiding the risk of going it alone is like standing at the pool-side watching others swim. You feel safe but isolated, yet testing the water is scary because the only way to master swimming is by surrender. The first step is learning to float. You have to trust, almost in defiance of common sense, that the water will support you.

Similarly, to follow your Life Mission means you let go of the support of others and learn to rely on the support of your Source (the same as you do with the water). When you cross the threshold of dependency on others and shake the feeling that nothing will be there to take its place, you learn that you will be held up by your Source.

When you risk embracing your Life Mission you are saying in effect, "I believe that I am doing the thing for which I was created. I am worth much more to myself and to the world by being me, rather than stay-

88

ing the person I am not. The only way to achieve my mission is to rely on my Source as the unabiding foundation of my being."

Risk validates your support of yourself. The paradox is, you risk everything by not being yourself. You can be strong only to the degree that you are willing to be yourself and rely on that self.

The Meaning of Risk

To risk means to move out of the familiar into the unfamiliar. It means leaving your safety zone and stretching onto the edge of new possibilities. If you're feeling secure, you'll be less motivated to try something new. When you are willing to forsake certainty for growth, you benefit. As an executive astutely said: "You have to recognize that every out-front maneuver you make is going to be lonely. But if you feel entirely comfortable then you are not far enough ahead to do any good. That warm sense of everything going well is usually the body temperature at the center of the herd. Warm fuzzies and risk do not mix." This chapter invites you to slip into something less comfortable and learn how to risk so that you can "achieve something grand," as Loewy put it.

Rewards of Risk

The payoff of daring to be who you are is enormous. Risk gives you a heightened sense of self, enabling you to explore and validate your authentic needs. *Remember that every time you risk it demonstrates that you are worth the effort.* What you gain is growth, development, and transformation. Risk can make you fearful because it sets an evolutionary process in motion which moves you inevitably toward transformation, including death. Only with the acceptance of death and transformation can you face life squarely.

Risk puts you in touch with your strengths. You realize that the comfort of living others' plans for you is an illusion and begin to live your own agenda. You'll increase your self-love and self-esteem by opting for authenticity (being who you are) and identify more of what you need. Finally, you'll learn how to risk living a life which gives you what you want. (Would you risk getting something you didn't want?)

First Steps

Learning how to take risks is an ongoing venture. There is no better antidote to depression and inertia in your Life Mission process than taking those first steps of risk. Sometimes the whole matter might look too over-whelming and huge to manage. One way to approach risk is to take the process apart and break it down into small chunks.

Sally's Trip

A silver-haired woman of sixty-three, Sally wanted to take a trip by herself, and had never dared to do so. A widow with two dogs, she had not travelled for ten years since her husband died. She spent her time sitting home depressed, hardly venturing out. Her husband had always done the planning, so she was terrified at the prospect of traveling on her own. I asked her to make a list of everything she feared about taking a trip.

Her list:
• Being alone and away for days
• Deciding where to go

90

- Being without my animals
- Finding my destination spot on the map
- Going to a library to read up on the location
- Calling up the travel agent
- Looking at checkbook to see if I can afford it
- Buying luggage
- Deciding how I want to get there (car, van, plane train)
- Identifying what special things I need, such as pills shots, special equipment.
- Investigating kennels for the dogs

I asked Sally to identify the scariest item on her list. To her surprise, she realized that her fears centered around leaving the animals. No one could take care of them; a kennel would be unthinkable. "Caging them up like that would be terrible," she insisted. Sally had allowed her animals to tie her down. She resolved to face her fears and investigated alternative ways to have the animals cared for and found a kennel where her dogs could run and exercise.

Sally's fear of travel had to do with that imaginary mental list she was carrying around with her, as you can see. Each item in itself was manageable (some more than others, of course). But by tackling the "worst" one on the list she got the ball rolling. By daring to risk, she finally visited a brother whom she had not seen for five years, continuing on from his Minnesota home to New York to visit a friend. Upon her return to Los Angeles, she vowed to herself that she would travel once a month. Her health and her emotional vitality improved.

*Exercise 5.1: BREAKING DOWN YOUR RISK
FACTORS*

It's easier and less imposing to begin with one
aspect of the risk process. Like Sally, identify
something you are afraid of risking. Then break
down the project or activity into its component
parts, selecting the key item you are having difficulty with.

1. Look at the one item you want to master. What
bothers you about it? Identify what steps you can
take to overcome your fear of this item. For Sally
it was how to cope without her animals. The solution: Sally took her dogs to a neighbor for a day.

2. Break your risk down into stages. For example,
if you are afraid to take a course at the university,
you could spend an afternoon walking around the
campus, read a book on the subject, attend a lecture, talk to a professor, or audit the course. Sally
went on a day trip by herself without her animals.

3. Make attitude changes. If you picked something which you simply don't like to do, how can
you change your attitude toward it? For instance,
if the details of a trip are a drag, like negotiating
with the travel agent, or doing research, can you
persuade a friend to help you with some of it?

4. Examine how the risk is going to benefit you.
Sally realized two things. First, she hadn't consid-
ered what she would do if she was hospitalized.
Thinking about her risk item made her aware of
the need to have an alternate care plan for her

animals. Second, she could see her brother, whom she missed.

What do you feel about your risk now? Is it so bad? I'll wager it looks halfway good.

Risk Is in the Eye of the Beholder

Often people assume something is a risk when it isn't. I quit a tenured position at a university, having waited much longer than necessary because I feared the consequences of that risk. There was no job to replace it and none in sight. Looking back on it now, I wondered what all the fuss was about. My assumption was that it was a risk to leave a secure job, whereas the real risk was to continue teaching at the university.

Valparaiso, Indiana, the town in which the university is located, is a hotbed of rest. It's a quiet, sleepy little conservative place which looks forward to the big event of the year, a popcorn festival. My life at the university consisted of preparing for classes, planning next year's courses and for relief, going on vacation. Without vacations I couldn't have faced the semester. It was, as St. Augustine said, my way of backing myself away from hell to get to heaven.

Today, I see my discontent and depression as clear clues I needed to leave. I felt depressed because I feared leaving a bad situation! And yet by labeling my departure a risk I had kept myself in fear of leaving for a good five years. It took three years to make the transition away from Valparaiso, but it worked because I dared to follow the vision of becoming who I already was instead of staying who I was not. I began to see that leaving was the only way to mental and emotional health. Above all, I saw that in order to get in sync with my Life Mission, I had to resign from my position as professor. At that point, leaving no longer seemed a risk.

Risk and Your PM

Some PM's will feel more comfortable with risk than others. Doers prefer it (but not emotionally), because they want to maintain power. Motivators avoid taking concrete action. Stabilizers fear change and sudden moves, hence they are reluctant to initiate. Analyzers do things only when they are sure they will be right; thus, decisions are risky for them.

Think about a risk you're reluctant to take. Is it on an emotional level? Saying a kind word to a boss you can't stand? Crying in front of one of your children or a mate? Showing your critical self? Saying what you really feel to someone you love or dislike? Exposing a vulnerable part of yourself? Or is it perhaps making a mistake at work, taking the initiative where others have always made the decisions, or just sitting back and listening when you know the answers already? Risk is a new behavior, but in the newness and the change you will invite growth.

Exercise 5.2: YOUR RISK QUOTIENT

Rate how you respond to the following statements, circling the appropriate number. If you agree strongly with a statement, circle #1; #2 if you agree; #3 if you are neutral; #4 if you disagree; and #5 if you strongly disagree. Add up the total.

agree⟨------------⟩disagree

1. I have to ask myself permis- 1 2 3 4 5
   sion before I risk.
2. I take risks only after every- 1 2 3 4 5
   thing else has failed.
3. I prefer to risk only the same 1 2 3 4 5
   kinds of things.
4. I investigate things thoroughly 1 2 3 4 5
   before doing them.
5. I am not an impulsive risk- 1 2 3 4 5
   taker.
6. I risk only when absolutely 1 2 3 4 5
   necessary.
7. My parents tended to make 1 2 3 4 5
   safe decisions.
8. I tend to do things in predict- 1 2 3 4 5
   able ways.
9. I don't laugh at myself much. 1 2 3 4 5
10. I care more about being right 1 2 3 4 5
    than taking action.
11. I don't like to structure my day 1 2 3 4 5
    a lot.
12. I try to fit in wherever I am. 1 2 3 4 5
13. I make a big deal out of little 1 2 3 4 5
    things.
14. I follow instructions and proce- 1 2 3 4 5
    dures easily.
15. I tend to accept the status quo. 1 2 3 4 5
16. I tend to go along with the 1 2 3 4 5
    group.
17. Questionnaires make me feel 1 2 3 4 5
    uncomfortable.
18. Change scares me a great deal. 1 2 3 4 5

19. I discourage others from taking risks.   1 2 3 4 5

20. I like to know what I'm getting into before I do it.   1 2 3 4 5

Total:_____

What Your Score Means:

20–30	You're probably scared to leave the womb
31–40	You leave the womb, but not the house
41–50	You always take an umbrella with you, except perhaps in Palm Springs
51–60	You haven't checked your spare tire in a while
61–70	You plan your vacation while on it
71–80	You often bet on dark horses
81–90	You never venture anything too soon
91–100	You notice the cliff after you've jumped off

If you score below 40, you ought to consider taking an assertiveness class in addition to the exercises below. If your score was between 40 and 60, the self-help methods we'll discuss should help you increase your score. If you score between 60 and 80, you will want to examine any areas where you have not yet risked and give them attention, and if you scored more than 80, you'll want to assess whether you take risks without first incubating your ideas.

Risk-Taking and Assertiveness

Risk-taking and assertiveness go hand in hand. A healthy approach is to protect and claim your own space. When you do, you're saying, "My behavior indicates I think as much of my space as others do." Here's how passive, assertive, and aggressive behaviors look:

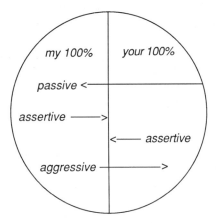

The circle represents the relationship between two individuals. Each is responsible for their own 100 percent (saying 50 percent would be more "logical," but does not carry the import of full responsibility). Aggressive behavior invades the other person's space. The person with passive behavior, on the other hand, allows the aggressor to enter their space. Assertive behavior says: "I am responsible for my 100 percent but not your half. I may be responsive to your half, but I am not responsible for it." Risk means claiming your space without aggressing upon another's.

You'll need this preparation for claiming a space of your own (your Life Mission).

To B. or Not to B.

Evelyn B., a quiet, shy secretary, illustrates how using assertiveness helps in taking risks for a Life Mission.

In the follow-up session to a workshop series, participants reported what things they had risked doing in
the intervening months.

Evelyn had changed her work process. She decided
to computerize her office's files even before she knew
how to operate a computer! Previously, when she
thought of doing anything new, she killed the idea by
telling herself the company wouldn't allow it or she
wouldn't allow it. She felt the frustration of files of
information piling up in the office, and knew there had
to be a better way.

Evelyn literally decided to assert her space, which
was difficult since she was a Systematic. Evelyn said
she had asked her boss for a computer then took four
weeks of company time to learn how to use it! This
meant going out on a limb in a big way for her. The
boss gave her little support, and the threat of being
fired "for taking so much time" loomed over her head
constantly. She kept her stance, worked on her 100
percent, and came up with a positive solution to the
office problem.

Now Evelyn's co-workers save valuable time in looking up and updating files by accessing the information
quickly. She was willing to take a leap in a manner she
had not done before. Her private risk was to tell herself
she could initiate a project at work. Her decision to
take responsibility for her own space gave her confidence and opened her up to a mission using technology
to improve communication and organization. The next
step was easy!

11 *How-To's for Taking Risks*

It's never too late to explore taking risks and going out
on your own personal limb. (After all, that's where the
tree bears fruit). The object is to get comfortable with

risks. Increase your risk-taking as far as you feel safe (but not TOO safe!). Here are some suggestions:

1. Review your risk process. Think back to the last time you risked something. What were the circumstances? What were you risking? What were your expectations? How did it turn out? What did you learn from the event? Would you risk in the same way again? Have you ever risked this way in your career?

2. Know what you want from your risk. So often something seems risky because you haven't the foggiest notion of the results you want. Be clear about your purpose in doing something, and take time to think it out first (especially good advice for Doers and Motivators). If you are unsure as to what results you want, list the worst and best outcomes possible. Probably what you want is somewhere in between. Write out the specific objectives based on your information and visualize yourself actually doing them. Evelyn's example points up an important factor in risk-taking.

Too often, people tend to stop themselves in mid-course, by interrupting a spontaneous risk-taking impulse. But if you know what you want out of a particular situation, you can risk more intelligently and minimize the likelihood of stopping in mid-stream. Remember when you were on the road taking wrong turns because you had no road map? Your Life Mission is that road map, a clearly defined need is the goal, and risk, the fuel to get you there.

3. Take a private risk. Start with something that has a good chance of turning out successfully. I suggest a private risk because the risk level is usually low. For example, a workshop participant said he had never before dared to wear a red tie to work! For him, a private risk might be to start wearing a dark maroon tie, and work himself up to red.

In a class once we shared private risks with each another. One participant reported that she went for an entire Saturday afternoon without a single agenda. Normally, she would fill up each minute with scheduled activities. For her it was outrageous, but no one knew about it.

4. Rehearse your risk. Rehearsal comes naturally to Stabilizers and Analyzers, who like to do things thoroughly, whereas Doers and Motivators need a run-through because they rarely prepare anything.

Pick a situation in which you want to improve the outcome. For example, let's say you bought a microwave, which turned out to be defective or not what you wanted. Review what you did about that situation which failed to meet your need. Maybe you simply lived with your purchase or took it back and got angry in the process. Redo the scene as you want it to turn out. Practice this mentally until it becomes comfortable.

The next time a similar situation occurs—say a washing machine doesn't perform as guaranteed—rehearse what you are going to say. Be sure that you have the result you want in mind before you begin. Try it out with a partner and role play it if you like. Get some feedback on how you're doing. That will help diffuse the sense of anxiety and give you confidence. Then go and carry through what you rehearsed. You'll put some steam in your self-esteem!

5. Encourage yourself. Boost your risk-taking ability by telling yourself all the things you admire about yourself. Practice doing it in front of a mirror. (That in itself is a risk!) Maybe one of your sterling qualities

100

is your empathic skill. By using it perhaps you can persuade the clerk to take back that defective item mentioned in the example above. Or perhaps you're funny. (You Motivators will tune into this.) You can also use your humor at the office when no one cracks a joke. For each risk that you take and get what you want, treat yourself to something as a reward. At all times be kind and gentle to yourself

6. Share your fears. Risk can be a lonely venture. Talk over with yourself any feelings of isolation you are experiencing. Give yourself space to experience any anxieties or worries, and discuss them with yourself. Admit to any fear so that you can work through it in the situation.

7. Accept failure as part of the process. Risk demands that we accept possible mistakes along the way. Edison documented hundreds of individual failures before he got the light bulb the way he wanted it. As one client put it, "If you've failed somewhere, you must be doing something right!"

If you stop taking risks because you fear failure, consider Jane. She was paralyzed by the thought of any kind of failure. The irony was that she had "failed" numerous times along the way! Among other things, she had flunked a certification exam, been fired from two jobs, and had a divorce. (She didn't yet realize that she needed to be free of those things.) Naturally I had to ask her why she was afraid of failure seeing as she was so good at it.

8. Ask if it's really a risk. Take a long hard look at the risk you're considering. Is it really a risk? Who says so? You or someone else? For example, if you didn't quit that job, how would your health be? If something is a risk, what are the alternatives of not carrying through with it? (Remember my example from Valparaiso.)

9. Take a risk with others. You don't have to risk everything alone. Clue someone in on your risky ventures. Get their support and feedback. Ask people about the risks they have taken. Read autobiographies of adventurers, explorers, pioneers, and risk-takers. Find out how they did it and the process of trial and error they went through. Their stories will give you encouragement. Paste up a picture of your heroes and scan the newspaper for stories of people you emulate and respect who have taken bold steps in their lives.

10. Recognize the risks you have already taken. Turn a piece of paper on its side, draw a horizontal line and put a hatch mark for every five years you have lived. Above the line, list at least four major decisions you made and reference each to the year the decision was made. Below the line, note what you feel would have been the result had you not made each particular decision:

Important Decisions I Made

Possible Result Had I Not Made Those Decisions

This exercise lets you see the risks you have taken in the choices you have made. Compare the person you chose to be (the top of the line) with the person you elected not to be (below the line). Give the exercise to a friend and ask them to describe both persons. What differences did you discover about the person you risked being? (The one above the line?) Who was responsible for the person you decided to be? Where would you be now if you hadn't taken the paths you did? Congratulate yourself for every decision. Each one shows that:

1) You were in control of your life.
2) You chose who you wanted to be.
3) You made some good choices.
4) You had definite reasons for doing what you did.
5) You took many risks!

EXAMPLE

Important Decisions I Made

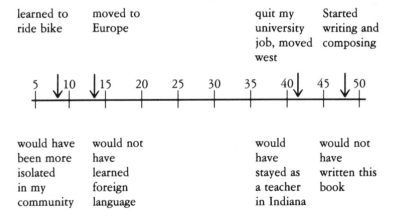

| learned to ride bike | moved to Europe | | | | | | quit my university job, moved west | Started writing and composing |

| would have been more isolated in my community | would not have learned foreign language | | | | | | would have stayed as a teacher in Indiana | would not have written this book |

Possible Result Had I Not Made Those Decisions

Were you surprised at how many risks you took?

11. Examine your past for risk takers. If you think you can't risk, look at your family history for examples of courage. Most of you who live in the United States are in this country because your ancestors braved new frontiers and followed their destiny, or were forced to come here against their will and risked their lives.

Everyone can find a tale of heroism and risk-taking in their heritage somewhere. Look for the pioneers, immigrants, or adventurers in your past and the risks they took! Ask your parents, grandparents, or other relatives to tell you stories of bravery in their memory. Get together with friends and share tales of courage from your respective family histories. These accounts will give you an added boost, instill you with pride and demonstrate the positive effects of taking risks. Give yourself this day your daily risk. It is your staff of life, your source of power, growth, uniqueness, and authenticity.

The more you risk, the more you'll say to your Life Mission: "I can."

Chapter Six

Eliminate Negative Thinking

If you say you can or you can't, you're right.

N egative thinkers are people who get up in the morning, see a molehill, and turn it into a mountain by nightfall. These nay-sayers get a lot of encouragement because negative thinking (= N.T.) is pervasive in our society. It's very difficult, for example, to find anything positive in the news or on TV; media executives are candid in admitting that disaster sells better than the "soft" (that is, more optimistic) human interest stories.

If you are blocked in your mission search, it could be that you're damming everything up with negative energy. N.T. keeps you from trying for the career you always wanted, daring your dreams, and realizing your Life Mission. Positive thinking enables body, mind, and spirit to accomplish your mission by giving you the

105

affirming confidence and faith in yourself that you need.

The goal of this chapter is to help you eliminate the debilitating effects of N.T. and replace it with positive, proactive thinking. You'll learn the causes for N.T., how to kick the N.T. habit and take charge of your thoughts. Remember, how you think is a self-fulfilling prophecy for every event in your life. If you say you can or you can't, you're right!

Comparing Positive with Negative Thoughts

Thoughts are things. They create energy fields. When you give thought a certain kind of energy, you attract that same kind of energy back to you. You receive exactly what you send out. Put another way, what you wish affects what you fish—and the kind of fish you get. Notice how you respond emotionally and physically to a positive story in the newspaper. It can actually make you feel better. Norman Cousins discovered the healing effects on the body when he induced laughter in himself during a severe illness.

The same equation is true of negative thoughts. If you see everything as negative, you will reap negative results. Thinking of things in terms of disaster diminishes and drains your energy. N.T. is every bit as destructive as poison.

You can demonstrate for yourself the debilitating effects of negative thinking on your body with the following experiment.

Exercise 6.1: YOU'VE GOT ME UNDER YOUR SKIN.

Get a friend who has not read this part of the book (in other words, before they buy *Finding Your Life Mission.*) Write down three sentences you are mentally going to say to this friend. Pick one negative and two positive sentences and the order in which you are going to say them. Example: 1) "Jane couldn't do anything right if she tried," 2) "Jane is the most wonderful person on earth," and 3) "Jane can be anything she wants to." Do not show these sentences to your friend.

Ask the friend now to hold one arm straight out to their side, and to resist any downward pressure you apply to it with two fingers of both hands. Apply pressure. Tell them you are now going to press downward three more times as you did in the practice attempt prefacing each attempt by saying "one, two, three."

Mentally say each sentence with your fingers resting on the person's arm and give the preparatory count. After saying "three," apply downward pressure as before. Watch for the difference in the resistance of your friend's arm between the negative sentence and the positive ones. Immediately after you think the negative sentence, your friend's arm will invariably weaken and you will easily push it down!

If you can make a person's muscles grow limp with N.T., imagine what a constant bombardment of such negativity can create over a period of time. Even worse, imagine what your N.T. will do to you in your mission search!

Let's return to **Exercise 5.1.** If you revert to thinking the positive sentence (without giving away your secret) your friend's arm will once again bounce back with strength to affirm your thought!

N.T.: The Sugar-Coated Pill

Why is N.T. so widespread? Why in the world would you want something that blocks you from your goals? Here are some reasons.

1. N.T. often gives a false payoff (sometimes known as secondary gain). For example, if you got ill as a child maybe you were subconsciously looking for your parents' attention. But there's the rub: the payoff might seem positive, but in order to get that attention, you have to diminish your capacities (i.e., get sick) to get it.

2. N.T. gives a cushion and protection from admitting you are wrong. If something you predict as "wrong" turns out that way, you won't have to blame yourself for being wrong! Your assumption that it was wrong all along, after all, is correct. Some people even unconsciously need the negative outcome to confirm their prediction. With this philosophy, you "win" when your negative prediction is negative. After all, you were right. Some victory!

If all of this seems a bit obscure, just apply it to an everyday situation. You're on the golf green. You tell yourself you are going to screw up. ("I know I won't make this putt.") When you in fact screw up, you may not like the results, but at least you were astute enough to predict them (I knew it all along!).

3. Negativity sounds so authoritative. N.T. frequently connotes realism, wisdom, clarity, and authority. For many, being realistic is proof of intelligence
and sanity! It also seems so mature! After all didn't
you learn N.T. more or less as an adult?

Positive thinking is associated with child-like naivete.
It is practiced by the gullible, dreamers, those in denial,
hedonists or the slightly loony. *Pollyanna* is the word
often used to describe an unrealistic, optimistic person.
Yuck!

Ways to Eliminate N.T.

Give your positive self the respect and attention it
deserves! GET THE N.T. OUT! Let's look at seven
ways to do it:

1. Acknowledge N.T. as an addiction.
2. Kick the habit by redirecting your energy positively.
3. Believe positive thinking will work. (**Pre-event approach**)
4. Use detached involvement: who knows if it's good or
   bad? (**Post-event approach**)
5. Accepting the process: aim where you hit.
6. Lose ugly N.T. in 30 days
7. Affirm your 30-day program daily.

You're aiming for one result: to remove any barriers,
blocks, and obstacles created by N.T. which keep you
from finding your Life Mission.

1. Acknowledge N.T. as an addiction. In spite of
the harmful side effects of N.T., it can have a stran-
glehold on you because it is just like alcohol, drug
abuse, or other addictive substances. An addiction is a
compulsive habit, like downer thoughts, predictions of

109

disaster, or finding fault. Negative thinkers grow dependent on them much like the substance abuser does with chemicals.

The unconscious works with the material you give it, accommodating your interpretation without objection. If you believe the letter you just got from the I.R.S. is a sure summons for an audit, your muscles will tense, heart pound, and adrenalin will secrete into your bloodstream.

Addictive N.T. throws up a giant wall between you and your goals, because each event is (pre)judged and diminishes your performance. (Try doing something productive in a physical and emotional state when you think the I.R.S. is after you). If, on the other hand, you open it without assuming anything, you'll be able to deal calmly with whatever the content is. It's all how you choose to apprehend the situation.

John's Stalled Self

John had built up a neat N.T. defense system to keep him from his passion for motorcycles. He was a small town Kentucky boy who had made it big in the city.

An account executive for twenty-five years, he had left his job and was looking for another one with similar pay (over $100,000 a year). John had yearnings for the outdoors, race cars, and a different life. *Easy Rider* and *Breaking Away* were favorite films of his.)

But his negative thinking critic went something like this: "Your constant need to tinker with machines, your fond memories of having driven a tractor at age 10 on the farm, and your passion for racing are not becoming of a grown man."

There was no breaking through the wall of doom around his desire. "If I become what I love to do, it will mean that I am selling out to something hokey.

Anyway, my hobby is not going to earn me money, and if I did what I liked, I'd go bankrupt." John preferred to be negative about what he loved so as to avoid embracing it. John truly "just said no" to his mission.

2. Kick the N.T. habit. Eliminating N.T. is a process of transformation. You can change N.T. into something which will work *for* you by learning to redirect your energy into something constructive. It's like harnessing electrical current, in and of itself neutral, for something which can be used effectively. (So go fly a kite, already.)

Kicking the N.T. habit begins with becoming aware of how dependent you are on negative thoughts racing through your head. Jot down some of your habitual mental tapes. Review them, and ask yourself what you would do if they suddenly stopped. What new behaviors would you have to adopt if your daily fix of N.T. were missing? Which N.T. have you been addicted to most?

Biology (Class) Is Destiny

A true N.T. addict, Glen was miserable if he didn't have his daily fix of N.T. Literally tied up in "nots," he could hardly say a sentence without a negative in it. Although his college work demonstrated a promising career in biology, Glen was convinced that for the rest of his life he was "doomed" to a high school teaching job showing students how to dissect frogs or collect butterflies.

But he was getting exactly what he wanted. Glen was like a fellow in a rain storm standing with a pole to attract lightning to himself. He had put all his energy into dreading the high school job, the location, even

111

what his miserable room would look like (with out-dated microscopes, dirty walls, and lackluster text-books). He had in fact attracted just the kind of job he was focused on. (What you resist persists.)

Glen monitored his negative tapes for several weeks and realized how he was dependent on them. Getting a job more true to his liking meant he would have to assume more responsibility for his thoughts. He began to shift his focus to what he wanted rather than what he feared, since fear resulted in negative thoughts.

Today, you'll find Glen happily working in a research firm. "The only butterflies I have to put up with now are before a research report is due." For the first time, Glen has a sense of fulfilling his mission of biological research on the immune system.

3. Believe positive thinking will work (pre-event approach). Beliefs are powerful agents. They help construct the reality you experience. You accomplish something only by truly and honestly believing it is possible. In order to stop N.T., you must have faith in what you are telling yourself. I call it using the #5 iron:

Strike While the (#5) Iron Is Hot

Annie, an avid golfer, once used her #3 iron at a driving range. Up until then she never believed she could hit the ball well with this iron. One day, she thought she was using her favorite club, a #5 iron Suddenly she noticed that she was actually using the #3 iron. Her good performance with that #3 iron happened because she believed she was using her trusty #5, with which she could do no wrong.

When I hear clients tell me exactly why a situation will turn out badly for them, I ask them why they are so sure, so fervent about predicting unfavorable results. I always urge them to use the same passionate belief to achieve positive results!

4. Use detached involvement. Who knows if it's good or bad? (Post-event approach). People use N.T. to anticipate an event not only proactively, as in the example of the #5 iron, but also *reactively* to judge an event after it is experienced. While the proactive approach is to think positively about upcoming events, the challenge in a post-event situation is *not to react at all*, but to see what can be learned so that the next event can be approached positively. I call this detached involvement. You play to win **(pre-event)** but are not attached to the outcome **(post-event)**.

There's an old Zen story which illustrates this detached involvement beautifully. When a man lost his horse, he responded, "Who knows if it's good or bad?" Shortly thereafter the horse returned with a mare. Now the man had two horses. His son rode the horse, was thrown from it, and injured his back. The man once again said, "Who knows if it's good or bad?" Soldiers of the local army came through the man's property, recruiting men for battle. The son could not go because of his injury. The father said, "Who knows if it's good or bad?" And so on the story goes.

Take any event which you reactively labelled negative at the time. But looking at it with hindsight, what did you learn from this situation? Many clients have interpreted a firing, job transfer, lay-off or the like as the universe's way of dropping not-so subtle hints. But, 60–70% of the people polled on their careers felt they went on to a better job after being fired. The word fired in itself is neutral. To be fired (up), for instance, is positive!

Learn to see events which have happened in a detached, neutral way. "Who knows if it's good or bad?"

Jovial Joan

> Joan was a 45-year-old businesswoman in the midst of a relationship break-up. Her once successful greeting card business had stalled, and she was up to her neck in personal debts. Tired of her old business, she didn't know what to move into. But something about Joan's attitude and demeanor was different. Always smartly dressed right down to matching eyeshadow to her blouse, her eyes sparkled with a refreshing zest for living, although she could have found dozens of reasons for doom and disaster thinking.
>
> Joan had a glowing, positive attitude about things. She knew her experience was for the good, knew things would turn out all right. Everything she did was in the context of her mission, to brighten people's lives through creativity and humor. She had the greatest faith in herself, even if she didn't know exactly which way to go at the time.
>
> She was stuck as a problem-solver, yet not mired in N.T. As she reviewed the reasons for her situation (she is a Motivator), she realized she had been too isolated in the past, needed to get out in the world, be more visible and use her verbal skills to promote a cause. (Detached involvement!) I told her to worry less about the specific outcome for now and concentrate on seeing just what turned her on. (See *Exercise 1.2)*

Now, a year later, Joan is negotiating a contract with a philanthropic organization where she can combine her skills as a businesswoman, art lover, and designer.

Does Joan have some access to a secret formula concocted by the ancients? Positive thinking did not prevent her from having "setbacks." But it was her attitude towards the events and her undying belief that everything was going to turn out just as it needed to which pulled her through. She believed in the ultimate wisdom of each event. It was the unshakable nature of her belief system which helped her shut out N.T.

5. Accepting the process: aim where you hit. Acceptance enables you to say, "the spot where my arrow landed was the one I had intended to hit all along," i.e., " I aimed where I hit." That's neither fatalistic nor defeatist. On the contrary, it affirms the rightness of any situation and that you will discover the wisdom of your experience.

If your car breaks down, and you have a negative reaction, then what are you telling yourself? My car (unlike any other car) ought not to break down. Things of this sort are unfair and do not fit my universal law #1, namely, "Nothing inconvenient or difficult should ever happen to me." Instead, look at why your car broke down and why you needed car trouble at *precisely* the time it occurred. Then you can approach the next situation positively with greater insight.

This discussion also pertains to traumatic events as well. Mary Louise Poor is a flutist who suffered a near-fatal automobile accident resulting in severe injuries including a collapsed lung and lacerations to her mouth and face. She spent 13 weeks in a hospital, three months in a body cast, and another six months on crutches. She has also resumed playing even though she has had to restructure the way she plays with a special mouthpiece. "Playing is not just my occupation and my life's work," she says, ". . . it's my being . . . it's part of my soul." She was able to carry on her mission in another form. She revised and redeveloped her skills and she has translated her mission into helping musicians who have suffered similar injuries.

No matter how terrible or devastating the situation might seem, reflect what you can learn from it. But do it without beating up on yourself by blaming yourself or others. (N.T.) There is a difference between acceptance of events and the belief that you deserved them or are being punished for them. When you insist on seeing yourself as victim, you abdicate the control you have over your life.

Friendly Persuasion

Although most of the emphasis in this book is on individual work, N.T is so pervasive that you can use supportive help from others. Because it is an addictive habit, a local Alcoholics Anonymous (AA), Al-Anon, Emotions Anonymous, Overeaters Anonymous (OA), or Adult Children of Alcoholics (ACA) would be ideal support groups to learn how to overcome addiction through the Twelve-Step Program.

You can also form your own network of people willing to work on encouraging positive thinking. (You could call it AINT—Anonymous Inveterate Negative Thinkers.) Here are some ways a group can be especially effective. Each person lists pet negative phrases, and then the group finds original or humorous alternatives to them. When you catch yourself saying your pet phrase, use the replacement suggested by the group. Group members can be supportive by reminding you if they hear you slip into your pet phrase—or any kind of N.T.

You can further discuss with the group the context in which you tend to use this negative phrase. Again, feedback from the group can help you realize how your N.T. is triggered. Finally, the group can also brainstorm to devise its own techniques and exercises for transforming N.T. into positive action.

Exercise 6.2: FLUSHING OUT YOUR NEGATIVITY

Write down all your negative equations surrounding a particular issue:

work	=	drudgery (not fun)
drudgery	=	good pay
pay	=	what I get for pain and suffering

Now rewrite the list in the most positive way you can. For example:

work	=	passion
passion	=	money
money	=	freedom
freedom	=	achieving my mission

Remember, you don't have to believe the list (yet), just jot it down and put it on your refrigerator! Now to the flushing part. Write down everything you feel negative about. Get all of those feelings OUT! Don't spare anything. If you dislike your kids, are negative about your mate, or hate the dog, ADMIT it on paper. Then, get rid of the list! You could a) burn it, b) tear it to shreds, or c) flush it down the toilet (if you've written it on toilet paper).

117

Be creative and invent your own way! One client eliminated his N.T. list by saying it aloud and expelling it in huge breaths after each item. You can imagine yourself releasing your N.T. like balloons drifting into the stratosphere. See them fade forever from view. They'll return from time to time, but you'll find that they diminish in strength or frequency of appearance. How would you like to keep showing up at a person's place where you are not wanted?

Each time you get new negative thoughts, gather them up as before and dispose of them in your favorite manner. Remember, this is a *constant* process. Just expelling the negative will in itself accomplish little if you fail to replace it with positive. Now that you are releasing your negativity regularly (isn't it nice to be regular?), you will find space opening up for the positive.

If you looked for red Dodge pickup trucks this week, you would start to see them everywhere because you directed your attention to them. What you look for is what you get. Apply it to positive thoughts, and anticipate them in your life! Actively look for good fortune to happen in your life. Every time it does, affirm that the universe has rewarded you for right action.

6. Get rid of ugly N.T. in just 30 days. N.T. should be thought of as crystallized thought patterns (and you know how hard a crystal is). It will come as no surprise that habitual behavior resists change rather vigorously. This exercise will help you get rid of ugly N.T. by means of a 30-day program using a different way of thinking.

Any crystallized N.T. must be transformed by a

fresh, vital, energetic, and softened mental system charged with a positive outlook. It will neutralize the acerbic and acidic effects of N.T.

Exercise 6.3: AROUND NEGATIVITY IN 30 DAYS

First, decide what N.T. issue you wish to transform. Perhaps you need to learn how to keep your home free of clutter, begin an exercise program, or improve your time management. State in a short, positive phrase exactly what you want. (You can identify important issues with the help of your most prevalent negative thought: "I can't ever seem to find anything." Change it to: "I need to organize my closets, files, or desk.")

Now write a second sentence which states the results you want. Make the statement short, to the point, in the present tense, and without any negations. "I want to be happier," or "I want some time to do what I wish," are vague and give your subconscious little to go on. If you say "happier" or "some time," how do you know when you have reached your goal?

Effective examples might be: "I want to reduce my cholesterol count by 20 percent" or "I want to have one hour of leisure time to write in my diary daily." These state clearly desired outcomes. Be sure you are detached from the outcome. This is what you want without any strings attached. A results-oriented sentence for issue #1 above might be: "I want to find anything I need in my closet, files or desk within one minute."

Say your results statement silently (or aloud if you prefer), each morning and night for a period of thirty days. If possible, devote five to ten minutes on each session. Make a contract with yourself to do the program daily. If you forget and skip a day, devote twice as much time to your issue the next day. If you skip two days, you must start over because the program is only effective on a continuous basis. You wouldn't diet or take antibiotic pills every other day, would you?

You may feel a certain amount of resistance, especially in the first few days, but don't give in to it. Stick to your program! You will begin to feel results in due time if you believe in what you are affirming.

Exercise 6.4: A LITTLE HELP FROM YOUR FRIENDS

Here's a final exercise which shows how to maximize your mission positively:

1. Write down the major things you intend to accomplish in your lifetime. You can use categories such as creative, financial, personal, material, spiritual, educational, or professional as guidelines.
2. Ask three friends to make the same list about you without having seen your version.
3. Now compare your list with theirs. What things did the friends think *you were capable* of that you did not?

Perhaps it's a matter of degree, like Jenny, who

was shocked to find out her friends thought she should go into politics and be a charismatic leader. "But I'm terrified to get up and speak in front of more than ten people!" she insisted. Then Jenny began to remember all those civil rights and Vietnam marches in which she had participated, and the big rally she organized for the ERA. She was up in front of people talking to them with no trouble! "I can't believe I convinced myself I couldn't do this for so long," she exclaimed, fighting back tears.

4. Now take one ability, talent, achievement your friend(s) say you are capable of. It does not matter if it is big or small. Just get it down on paper! Then complete the following:

*As my friend has recognized, I am able to*_____
_____*(friend's words). Yes, the truth is, I am very capable of*_____*(put in your own words).*

Therefore, I am going to give positive energy to achieve
_____ *(what you intend to do).*

Resolve to make your statement materialize, no matter how major or minor it is. Be passionately involved in the success of your goals! When you go through this program of eliminating addictive N.T., of affirming the positive, of believing in and watching for the positive to transpire in your life, you can expect the riches of the universe that are rightly yours. Surprising things will happen!

Your Life Mission will become a reality when you say "I can."

Chapter Seven

Anticipate the Unusual

*S*urprise!!!

When you hear that word, you know something fun or unexpected is going to happen. That's why science fiction, whodunits, fantasy films, clever jokes, and dreams are so popular—they all contain unusual, weird, or bizarre events.

Real life, however, is another matter. Many people have days so characterized by routine and predictability, that you know exactly what they're going to be doing at 3 P.M. Even worse, 3 P.M. for them seems about the same as 3 A.M. They're here today—and here tomorrow.

If you are one of those who is bored with what you are doing but can't get out of the rut, if you feel you've had about as much of yourself as you can take, if you think you are boring yourself, then this chapter is for you.

We'll discuss the ways to be the architect of a vibrant and thrilling mission by injecting more of the surprising, the offbeat, and the amazing into your life. This chapter will be especially valuable for Analyzers (who look for rules) and Stabilizers (who look for precedent), but also for Doers (too much in a rush) and Motivators (who are the most comfortable with the unusual).

"What'll You Have?" "Oh, the Usual..."

People often have dull existences, dreary jobs and relationships because they anticipate the usual—in fact, they actually expect it. If life is nothing special, then it is difficult to view a Life Mission as special. A humdrum existence does not foster an exciting life.

Viewing things as "business as usual," stops the flow of process and prevents you from experiencing life in its variety and richness. Life becomes one-sided, monotonous, and lacking in options. You learn nothing from sameness.

We'll turn now to a discussion of three detractors of the unusual: conformity, the commonplace, and control, and to its three attractors: change, creativity, and context. The former will show how you build up barriers against the unusual. The later will offer ways to remove those obstacles.

Detractor #1: Conformity

The problem with a "usual" life is that you must follow all the rules and conform to prescriptions. That will ensure nothing unusual. The results are as sure as betting on rain in Seattle. Conformists expend a lot of

123

energy maintaining and protecting their beliefs, thereby shutting out change and variety. They pursue the straight and narrow to the point of exhaustion. Conformity demands sameness without exceptions, while the unusual is by definition an exception to the rule. A belief system which tries to conform on all levels is an illusion.

By adhering to unbending points of view, conformists unwittingly contradict other beliefs they hold. Example: "Long hair in women is okay—but not in men"—while a picture of Jesus hangs on the their wall. Or, "It's okay for someone to be gay as long as they don't actually talk about it," while at the same time they believe that "it's a sin to tell a lie."

And on the contradictions go. Rigid beliefs clash with each other like bumper cars at the local fair. The usual feeds on conformity, rules, rigidity, whereas nonconformity doesn't like confining "rules" (which don't mesh with each other anyway).

Detractor #2: Control

Anne Wilson Schaef in her book, *When Society Becomes an Addict* (Harper & Row, 1986), talks of the pervasive illusion of control in our society. "We feel as if we must control, because we do not have inside ourselves what we need . . ." The need to control adversely affects a Life Mission in every way! If you've got it all mapped out, why bother?

Control prescribes rather than describes events. It's like the coach who tells the team: "I expect you to win. And here's how you are to do it. In the third quarter, Smith will pass to Jones at exactly 3:52 into that quarter, and Jones will cross the goal line at a spot three yards and 10 centimeters from the edge of the

124

playing field." Sound ridiculous? Sure, but it is no less exact than many of my clients who predict *for sure how something is going to happen before they've even tried it.*

You can't control how a child, a vacation—or life is going to turn out, so stop trying to do it! Concentrate rather on letting what is inside you unfold and let yourself be surprised!

Detractor #3: The Commonplace

Familiar things are the antithesis of the unusual. Symbols such as McDonald's arches, the Best Western sun symbol, or Campbell's soup are popular because you know what you are getting—a similar, if not the same experience. (Andy Warhol played upon this sameness in his Campbell soup paintings.)

The commonplace rarely affords you the opportunity of encountering something different. It's like using English abroad rather than trying a few phrases in a foreign language. Will it be McDonald's or that cute little café where they only speak Flemish?

On the other hand, when you eschew the commonplace, you welcome change. "I don't know what I am getting, and that's okay." (Not recommended, however, for Bulgarian restaurants with incomprehensible menus, where I once ended up with a chicken replete with head and claws.) Growth comes from experiencing differences. Sameness begets only itself.

The Common Path to Routine and Ruts

Familiarity breeds content! The same route to work, food for lunch (McDonald's anyone?), radio station, work pattern at the office. You don't really have to think because everything happens on automatic pilot.

125

No wonder, then, that you're reluctant to explore, when routine and sameness are so enticing. And, of course, doing things in a routine way saves you from experiencing *yourself* in another context.

Missions suffer from much the same miring in ruts and routine as do everyday activities. Many clients complain of their lives and jobs being too predictable, too boring and too much of the same, all of which indicates a need for stimulation. But people continue to stay in what they know (the rut) rather than deal with what they do not know (the unusual).

Routine is not always bad. Certain activities lend themselves to a ritualistic approach, such as cleaning out the bird cage, shifting gears, or brushing teeth. The only problem with routine is when it goes unchallenged. Useful as a means to an end, routine must nevertheless be re-examined from time to time. Ever driven to work and wondered how you got there? Hoped you hadn't run someone over without even noticing? It's compulsive, unconscious habit which needs monitoring because it dulls your Life Mission search and robs you of directly experiencing the present.

Routine Ways to the Unusual

Ironically, routine is the starting point for getting out of ruts and anticipating the unusual. The following exercise will give you the opportunity to change things you are very familiar with and don't think much about.

Exercise 7.1: THERE'S GOTTA BE ANOTHER WAY.

Take any daily activity and figure out another way to perform it. Start simple and mundane. Maybe it's the way you shop in a supermarket, swing your tennis racquet or fry eggs. If you practice your tennis serve for ten minutes with your non-serving hand you'll discover all sorts of things about your PM you didn't realize. (And your serve will improve.)

You can also redesign an ordinary object in another way. I once asked workshop participants to analyze a common desk calendar. How did the calendar interpret time? For example, what was important, daytime or night? Weekdays or weekends? Was it work- or pleasure-oriented? Was it present- or future-oriented?)

Then participants were to design a calendar that expressed their own concept of time. One person reduced week days to one forth the size of the weekends; another gave each day a different color; a third changed the days to the size of a postage stamp, while giving the evenings a larger space. One woman made her days all gray and narrow, and realized that her job depression was due to a feeling of restriction and imprisonment. She needed greater expansiveness and excitement in her life. An unusual calendar made the oblivious obvious.

Attractor #1: Change

If you can do just one thing out of the ordinary today, you will experience the benefit of change. Change involes risk, growth, adventure, exploration, and new-ness; all are fertile ingredients for nurturing the un-usual. Where there is conformity, change is stifled. Anticipating the unusual comes from the willingness to consciously alter old patterns.

Change helps break ordinary patterns—those which we all fall into from time to time. When you say: "I can't do anything about it," that means you feel it's impossible to break the pattern of sameness. That's just the problem. People fear change and think they have no power to effect it.

Dreams are also proof that you have the innate ca-pacity to imagine and engineer new and extraordinary things. I've never had—or heard of—a dull dream.

Attractor #2: Creativity

Anticipating the unusual is a creative act and must be practiced continuously. If you wait for the unusual to happen instead of creating an environment for the un-usual, you'll be unprepared for dealing with a truly unusual situation. Waiting until you are in the throes of an unusual event is too late. Your creative self looks better when you are prepared.

But how can you program yourself in advance to re-spond to something unusual? By being loose and flexible. Like a tennis player, you need to be prepared to bounce in any direction to hit the ball. That's why these players stay light and bouncy on their feet, ready to go a num-ber of ways. But if you program yourself to go only to the right, in other words be fixed, rather than creative in your response, you will not master an unusual play. Creativity is the means to respond to the unusual.

We need new ways to perceive and respond to sit-uations. Responses cannot be pre-programmed, only practiced and anticipated. What so often happens in crisis situations is that people react with routine, patterned, and repetitious responses. Being able to handle the unexpected in a situation has to do with the intention and ability to recognize the unusual in everything. Only then can you generate options rapidly and easily when they arise.

The paradox is that the unusual must be an everyday event, yet always be unique. Berthold Brecht created situations in his dramas which forced the audience to remember they were in a theater. He attempted to destroy illusion with his so-called *Verfremdungseffekt* (alienation effect). For example, the theater-goer was invited to "sit back and smoke," actors talked to the audience directly, and banners announced what was going to happen. Brecht wanted to jolt people out of the lethargy of the "four walls" of the theater, in which they "lose" themselves in the play. In the same way, we need to see the theater of our own lives with the same alert, conscious awareness.

Exercise 7.2: STALKING THE STRANGE

1. Make up your own mind games which force you to see things from another (and therefore unusual) perspective. Put one noun each on a slip of paper, put them into a hat, and draw out three slips at a time. Invent a story with the three words, and establish a connection between them. (Authors practice this method when they take three characters and weave them into a plot.)

For now, use the words hat, string, and baby rattle to create a story.

129

2. Be on the alert for the strange in any situation. An unusual feature in the Iran/Contra Hearings of 1987 was that most of the participants wore ties in various shades of red. Now this color has become routine for politicians—and broadcasters, too (especially those who want to become politicians). Keep a log of unusual things you see and read. Observe how your ability to see and attract offbeat things increases.

3. Get books with exercises and mind puzzles. Devote a period of time each day to work on them. Make up your own games and try them out on others.

4. Observe how cartoonists feed on the unusual to make you laugh. Practice writing new captions for their cartoons. (Don't peek at the cartoonist's version.)

5. Do anything you can to force a change of perspective on an issue. If you are in agreement with someone, you learn very little that is new or unusual. If you are in favor of amnesty for aliens, take the other side and defend that position. Or pretend you are Gloria Steinem being asked to debate on the merits of defeating the Equal Rights Amendment.

6. Record your dreams as examples of your own built-in fantasy factory. The unusual is usually there if you look for it!

Attractor #3: Contexts

You can wake up knowing something refreshingly different is going to happen by deciding to make it happen. What you wish affects how you fish! (And the kind of fish you get.) You'll even discover your dreams can become more fantastic. You shape and define a situation by the way you see things. The event occurs according to the situation you are in. That's a context.

Life is not meant to be lived in a boring context. The unusual thrives on your willingness to step out of a comfort zone (something I talked about in Chapter 5). It's up to you to create suitable contexts in which the unexpected can thrive.

People love to travel so much because it allows for surprise—often of the humorous variety. One day I was frying an egg in my dormitory kitchen in Germany. I was well aware that Germans only eat eggs sunny-side-up. As I turned the egg over, the German student cooking next to me announced in shock, "You just turned your egg over!" The student had never seen a fried egg "over-easy."

Shaping Contexts

Your mission depends upon the context you create. Here's an example of how you might do it. In a drama class, we were given an exercise to pick an emotion and then look for it in everything we saw, felt, or experienced for the next ten minutes. My choice was humor. Looking around the room, I began to see all kinds of odd things which had escaped my attention: the strange way people sat, funny props backstage, humorous conversations people were having. Even my own body seemed comical to me after a while. I found myself repeating the same word (tuna) over and over until it became hilarious.

Other people in the class picked very different emotions, and although they had the same surroundings, they experienced things in the way they had programmed them. Some responded to their context with tears, others with anger, still others with depressing silence. Thus a funny setting for one person may be interpreted by another as angry or depressing.

The variations one can generate are endless. But sadly, most people opt for unchanging and closed-ended contexts. If you stay within defined boundaries, unaware of your fenced-in approach, you create a dull life. Your mission will follow suit.

Look in the mirror, steam it, and trace the outline of your head. You might have assumed both your real and "mirror" heads were the same size (unless you've done this little exercise before). Surprise! You'll discover the mirror version is about half the size of your "real" head. But how could you become aware of it on your own? Only by looking for the out-of-the-ordinary, by taking nothing for granted (nothing as expected). Everything depends on how you choose to view it. Anticipating the unusual requires an expectancy that surprise is everywhere to be found.

Expectancy vs. Expectations

Think about the meaning of "You get what you expect." It's used almost exclusively to refer to negative or unfavorable outcomes, and functions much like watching a videotape of a sporting event. If you know the outcome to the game, there are no surprises. Expectations by definition deny the possibility of the unexpected. With expectations you assume you are in the driver's seat and that you know what the best solution is for every situation.

I remember the first time I went to Los Angeles. I expected the city to be tacky, smoggy, and full of traffic. I believed, as W.C. Fields remarked, the only thing which belonged in L.A. was an orange. I didn't want to be that orange. I could taste, feel, and see smog everywhere. (Where else do you get the luxury of seeing what you're breathing?) But it was December when pollution levels were relatively low for Los Angeles. In fact, there was no unusual (!) smog activity for that particular day. But I expected the negative stuff, and I got what I bargained for.

Expectancy: Getting What You Don't Expect

Expectancy differs from expectations in that you are open to outcomes rather than controlling them. The latter focuses on products and results, whereas expectancy focuses on surrender to the unfolding process. You plant seeds, set the stage, and allow (release) your work to happen in its own way. You achieve expectancy by injecting surprise and wonder at what will transpire.

Expectancy makes life exciting and easy because you can replace pushing with pulling and attracting what you want. Expectancy approaches life with an anticipatory rather than a controlling attitude. Of course, it's important to prepare for what you want and to do your groundwork (context!). If you want corn you plant corn, but leave the maturation process to nature.

The French: Legion for the Foreign (Context): Dancing In and Out of Contexts

Let's look at the successful way a French film crew practiced expectancy in their documentary. The subject was small-town American life. From my American perspective, the subject matter was very familiar: birth, death, picnics, work, family life, lazy pace, people puttering in gardens, and gossiping over backyard fences. Life seemed pretty ordinary and things didn't change much from year to year. I wondered what the audience would find interesting about this film. (Would a documentary on your life yesterday have been interesting material to document?) Then I began to look at small town USA from the perspective of the foreign crew. What did they find so intriguing and different about our way of life? Suddenly I had an important insight. The French crew could see the unusual almost right away, I had to actively LOOK for it. How come?

I had to consciously look for the unusual because I was only seeing a familiar American town, and had never practiced looking at it differently. The crew, on the other hand, had placed themselves outside of the context that they were familiar with—their French context—crushing wine with their feet, searching for truffles with pigs, sitting for long periods over café au lait in bistros. They anticipated seeing something different. The film as it unfolded was the difference. Here's how the process looks:

Expectation	*Result*
(CONTROL) you define outcome of context, push, make happen	no guarantee of benefits

Expectancy	*Result*
(SURRENDER) you do not define outcome of contest, allow to happen	you always get what you need

Going APE

I tested out my theory of expectancies in a creativity workshop. Participants were asked to go "APE" over something: that is, to develop the Attitude of Poised Expectancy about something and then focus on it without expectations. I encouraged them to select something which they felt was possible, reasonable, and quantifiable. (Seeing a Martian might have been too fantastic, five wart hogs too unrealistic, and seeing Beethoven in the form of a cloud somewhat hard to prove.)

They had only one rule to follow: program not how something was to happen but that it would happen. And, they had to desire and believe that this something would happen without defining how or how much. One participant simply noted how many red trucks, if any, she saw in a week. She reported thinking there had to be a preference for red pickup trucks in her neighborhood, because she began to see them everywhere—twenty-seven in all!

One participant decided to see how many nickels she would find in one week. Easy choice, you say? Well, she excluded the ones in common places in her house (dresser, jar, kitchen table). She began to find them on the street, in her file cabinet, and in her toilet bowl! The amazing thing was, she casually told her niece about the project in a long-distance call, and her niece began finding nickels everywhere, too!

A nice bonus to all this: At the office this person also found things for which she had been looking for over six months! (Remember what I said about rewards?)

A third participant went APE over finding playing cards on the street and told the group he would bring in the results the following week. After that class he found four outside his car in the company parking lot, and the next week he found eleven on the street at once (precisely the correct number for a tarot reading—which he happened to do regularly).

The importance of the exercise is not to make coins appear magically or put some hex on playing cards. The real lesson is a paradox: Things happen because you look for them, but not necessarily when you are looking for them. Discovery is only possible when you least expect it! The same is true for your mission.

desire (express)	>	*belief* (trust)	>	*focus* (commit)	>	*release* (surrender)	>	*manifestation* (expectancy)

Exercise 7.3: WISHING WELL

Step 1: Identify what you want without guilt or hesitation. "This is my desire and I own it."

Step 2: Trust that your choice is appropriate and that you will release doubt.

Step 3: Stick to what you have selected, refusing to let yourself get sidetracked or tempted to give up on your goal.

Step 4: Relinquish your impulse to work on the issue by controlling the outcome in any way.

Step 5: Invoke the law of expectancy. Watch, rather than control, the outcome. It's akin to bearing a child: you initiate the process, but you don't know exactly how the child will develop.

Let's look at how Andy applied expectancy to finding his Life Mission.

Andy's Angst

An executive in the direct-mail business, Andy stumbled into that field after going through a number of jobs, all of which he "fell into." A rather brash and cocky guy, Andy assumed things would come his way whenever he wanted to make changes. But somehow the magic he hoped for never materialized. Of course, since the direction he had taken in business had little to do with his mission, how could there be that magic?

Andy had always secretly wanted to promote personal growth through sports, yet he was convinced his mission was too "weird." He felt he was past the age of being an athlete. That stemmed from his "logical," rut thinking.

Andy needed to release seeing his sports mission as "strange." First, he went APE over anything which crossed his path combining sports and personal growth, and during that process, he completed the exercises below. (We'll come back to the outcome of Andy's story later.)

Exercise 7.4: FROM FAMILIAR TO STRANGE . . .

a) Open a newspaper and look at an action photo until it becomes strange, silly, or weird. Furnish a new caption or scenario for the picture to describe your viewpoint.

b) Exaggerate "fixed" things. Victor Borge has done this with his inflated language. In this language, a tuba becomes a "fourba;" forget becomes "nineget" after inflation. Imagine what it would be like if everybody had ten-inch-fingers. Or three heads. Then think of variations you could use for parts of the body in old songs: "You Go to My Heads," "I've Got You Under My Armour," "Moonlight and You in My Tendrils."

c) Devise inventive ways to transform a familiar object into an unusual one. For instance, your coffee cup. What else could it be? (The earring of a giant.)

d) Look at things as if you were a member of the other sex. How would you express yourself, walk, or gesture? What secret things would you do that you don't do now—and what things could you do after this exercise that you resisted doing because of your expectations? Practice walking around, talking, or gesturing in the manner you described in the privacy of your own home. (If your loved ones begin to react strangely to your antics, you could say that you were rehearsing for a local theater production of *Victor/Victoria*.)

e) Look for unusual combinations which you don't normally associate with each other: the elderly and day care (there are now day care centers for seniors). Find examples which capitalize on creative combos, like babies and sunglasses (used in the ad for the movie *Raising Arizona*), which capitalize on unusual or humorous combinations. In fact, advertising is a particularly rich source for strange combinations.

f) Now think about a familiar career and see if you can describe it in a bizarre, humorous, or unusual way. Example: A computer programmer could be a person who organizes and controls how people move their fingers across little square keys to get information.

Exercise 7.5: ... AND BACK

In addition to sprucing up the ordinary, we need occasionally to demystify the exotic. We'll reverse the process and go from the uncommon to the common. This part is especially useful for those of you, like Andy, who can't accept their mission because it's too strange or too far out for words. Get rid of equations and categorized thinking. Weird is more likely in the eye of the beholder. Instead, look at your mission with a new vision, accepting it first on its own terms for what it is, as just there. You can accept what's there as possible, right? (Except Gertrude Stein, who felt there was no there there.)

1. Look at something quite strange, and turn it into something ordinary. You can fantasize why creatures created by Gary Larson or Charles Addams might think of themselves as quite ordinary. In fact this is part of the humor Larson uses—they're just folks. Creatures from outer space might think we're weird, without three eyes, tentacles, or diamond-shaped head(s).
2. What in your family is actually a bit uncommon but you always thought was normal? Observe how often people talk about "strange" things in their families. (In one client's case, his father stayed at home, and his mother worked outside the home. This was in the late 1940s. He was in for a surprise when he went to school and found out almost everyone thought it was weird.)
3. Take what you think is an "offbeat" career,

139

one maybe you have even fantasized about, and describe it as "ordinary." Artist: shrinks people and things by putting a whole landscape onto a 4' x 6' piece of canvas.

    4. Read about "weird" missions people have and make them ordinary. Some from my scrapbook include: knowing everything about the potato, manufacturing soap while preaching religion, collecting obscene words in every language.

Perhaps, in the example of the computer programmer, it gives a sense of the power to provide people with access to information. With the artist, on the other hand, the process is perhaps not so mysterious as you might think.

Remember Andy the athlete? Soon after doing the exercises outlined above, a friend came to him with an idea for starting hiking and exercise workshops for adults who were recovering from illness or surgery. Now he could accept something he previously would have thought weird, and it awakened his slumbering mission. And now, of course, he was using the mail-order experience to promote his new endeavor. . . .

Whatever you come up with to describe a mission in a different way furnishes a fresh view. Doris felt she was an "ordinary" secretary. What mission was there in that?

Doris Directs

Doris was a woman of unbelievably positive energy and organizational talent. A Doer/Motivator, she had whipped her office into shape after only one week on the job. She got away from her commonplace view of being a secretary by describing her job in a creative way. She painted a colorful scene, seeing herself as a combination of traffic cop, air controller, and railway station engineer. Everyone had to stop in front of her desk, nothing could really move forward until she gave the signal. Doris switched one person to another on the phone, sent out and received information from near and far, facilitated traffic flow, determined who was to arrive (with a call), and when.

"I'm a giant mood motivator," she quipped. The cheery tone she set affected the office, as if she had slipped the staff pills in their morning brew to influence how she wanted the office to behave. She realized her enormous power for motivating people. She also felt much better about her contributions in her job, and began to appreciate how much she was needed. After this exercise she asked for a raise and got it! She began to recognize that her calling involved being a kind of human relations theater manager/set designer who prepared the stage for maximum performance.

To recap: If your life needs sprucing up, if it's "just like everything else and nothing special," rewrite the script into something more fantastic, unique, or inventive! You are responsible for co-creating that script. It does not happen on its own.

Adding the unusual to life makes it spicier, richer, and more stimulating. Life is not meant to be dull and drab, so give it drama and excitement! In order for life to have twists, you must change the way you approach it. Surprise yourself daily with your own creative additions and ingredients. Invite, await, anticipate, be expectant of a marvelous life!

Yeast your mission with novelty and growth.

Chapter Eight

Tolerate Ambiguity

Hamlet: Do you see yonder cloud that's almost in shape of a camel?
Polonius: By the mass, and 'tis like a camel, indeed.
Hamlet: Me thinks it is like a weasel.
Polonius: It is backed like a weasel.
Hamlet: Or like a whale.
Polonius: Very like a whale.

—SHAKESPEARE, *Hamlet*

Nature allots time for things to take shape before a process is complete. It is a period of time for an entity, not yet fully formed or shaped, to develop. Take butterflies, for example. During their cocoon stage, they are actually liquid for a while.

Ambiguity is like that fluid period. Just like the butterfly, you, too, must traverse a formative, ambiguous phase of a process to reach mental clarity in your mission search. The goal is to achieve focus and certainty in your mission. The way to certainty requires that you first tolerate any ambiguity required in the process for your thoughts to take shape.

By undergoing ambiguity, you can look at a situation honestly and without prejudgment, before it is complete. Ambiguity operates on its own terms and permits your imagination to open up to new possibilities. It allows time for play and creativity, when you can fool around, speculate, maybe change your mind, or just toss ideas back and forth. As Hamlet and Polonius said to each other: camel, weasel, or whale? It really doesn't matter. It's fun to play with possibilities!

An ambiguous phase can be scary, because it's fuzzy, loose, elusive, slippery—even confusing or chaotic. It's like a jigsaw puzzle. The pieces lie scattered helter-skelter at first. They don't fall into place immediately. But gradually the picture emerges.

The same process is true of your mission, too. You take things in, without judgment or comment, re-arrange the pieces this way or that, until you see a picture emerging.

In this chapter, you'll learn how to tolerate ambiguity by developing flexible thinking, suspending assumptions and prejudgments (which block desires and restrict options). Your goal is to clarify your mission.

Ambiguity and Your PM

The word ambiguity means "going on both sides." Put another way, it means not taking sides *for the moment*. Doers and Analyzers are most uncomfortable with that notion. They find it difficult to release control. Those who tolerate ambiguity agree that not getting there immediately is part of the fun (very appealing to Motivators). They need to take that delicious opportunity to be flexible, explore, and discover by refraining temporarily from making decisions.

Analyzers and Stabilizers have difficulty with ambiguity because of their preference for predictability. Analyzers have the greatest need for clearly defined answers. For Stabilizers, procedure and logic are all-important. They represent the methodical approach to life. Doers head straight for fastest results (witness Lois), and tend to bypass any nebulous phase. (Many Doers I know would have preferred to skip the womb and enter life full-blown out of the head of Zeus.) Motivators appreciate ambiguity, but they need practice moving beyond it and on to clarity.

Being Clear about Tolerating Ambiguity

Ambiguity enables you to create possibilities. There is a professor at a California university who offers a course in fuzzy thinking. Imagine! Encouraging chaos and ambiguity before designing a high-rise!

Phillip Davis and David Park in their book *No Way: The Nature of the Impossible*, point out that a major task in becoming a physician is to accept the impossibility of ever being sure. Tolerating ambiguity means being comfortable with the assurance you don't yet know it all.

The more you operate with foregone conclusions without allowing for any other approach, the more your Life Mission will be one-dimensional. Those who cannot tolerate ambiguity have everything figured out in advance. They remind me of the man standing in front of me at the movies, talking about the film he was going to see: "Whatever it's about, I'm certain I won't like it." His mind was made up.

In the previous chapter, I discussed the difference between expectations and expectancy. Ambiguity is a kind of expectancy. It puts emphasis on process, development, and surrender. Expectations are like a parent saying: "That's the way it's going to be and that's that!"

Lois Closes

Lois is a good example of closing off her mission options out of fear of ambiguity. Strong, high-spirited, and independent-minded, she resembled a cross between Eleanor Roosevelt and Babe Zaharias, with a pinch of Italian opera flair thrown in. A chip off the old block, she went about life in the same tough-minded way as her father, a naval officer. A Doer, Lois preferred getting on with things, rather than mulling them over.

Lois had always had a mission she wanted to pursue, but used all her marvelous energy to check it by carrying around a clear list of reasons (assumptions) why her calling wouldn't work. At twenty-nine, she was, not surprisingly, headed for boredom and burnout. "But," she declared, "I'll stay with my nursing job, the 'correct' thing to do for a woman, because the passion I have for the ocean means going back to school, loss of income, and stiff competition." None of her reasons were rational.

She knew for certain she was going nowhere, and also knew "for certain" that where she wanted to go was impossible. Unlike St. George, Lois preferred to generate dragons rather than conquer them. Her mission was **omission**,—she couldn't tolerate ambiguity, she wanted her life neatly wrapped, clear-cut, and absolutely defined. Lois didn't have two sides to go on— she really had none.

A Way Station to Clarity

Seekers of the truth know there are way stations along any continuum—all the points between A and Z. Tolerating ambiguity allows you to tarry along those way stations for observation, reflection, and eventual clarity. Part of the fun is the whimsical and unstructured period of the process. Let me make this perfectly clear: *premature closure can reduce options or restrict choices.* The path to certainty is often cloudy and needs time for focusing. Ambiguity allows a temporarily blurred picture to work in your favor by making the right choice apparent on its own.

Obstacles to Ambiguity

Fear and rigidity are two major barriers which prevent people from tolerating ambiguity. Fear of ambiguity results from an inability to release control or to suspend the need for clarity. It often creates anxiety because ambiguity requires you to defer for now the wisdom which will come later. When you are in quicksand, the temptation is to struggle, when in fact the best thing is to release control temporarily.

It would be absurd to preface looking at clouds by saying: "I know exactly what I'm going to see," or "There's no use doing this because I'm not going to see anything anyway." Yet many people use similar controlling statements about their Life Mission. No fuzziness, please.

Exercises with the greatest ambiguity have the most anxiety-producing effect on those whose thinking is rigid. Such people usually ask, "What's the purpose?", "What's this leading to?", "How am I supposed to do it?" These questions reveal a rigid, prescribed way of thinking. A mission is not a granite block, immutable and unmovable. It requires pliable thinking.

Martha, like Lois, illustrates the pitfalls of defining everything rigidly. She showed a high degree of artistic interest, but because she had little practical experience in the arts, she felt that admitting these interests "doomed" her to becoming a poet, painter, or potter. And these stereotypes were fixed in her mind:

Martha's Made-Up Mind

A prosperous and impeccably dressed suburbanite in her late forties, Martha was struggling with a nameless hankering, a sense of boredom or ennui, in spite of her beautiful home in Malibu and her two scholastic-minded teenagers. She had not felt the need to generate her own income because her husband had a high-ranking position in a large downtown law firm.

Like many of her suburban friends, she had served enthusiastically in a number of volunteer capacities, art shows, and local library fund-raisers, but all of this community service was wearing thin. Martha's testing indicated that she was attracted to art but when she thought of the word artist she had all sorts of preconceived definitions. I asked her to list what "artist" meant for her.

STOP! (Before you read on, do the following exercise):

Exercise 8.1: MY EQUATIONS

Make your own list of what the word "artist" means to you (type of work, age, environment, financial situation, location, ethnic background, political leanings, and so on). Then compare your lists with Martha's. Hers included:

147

male
painter
living in loft
pitiful
small disheveled apartment
poor
dedicated
in poor health
alone
apolitical

Martha had kept her artistic interests neatly suppressed, and it's easy to see why. Her view of an artist's life was rigid. For her, that lifestyle meant starvation, a lonely existence in a drafty loft apartment, with no chance for obtaining a dream house or feeding his child. (Her artist was male, to boot—not much chance of her becoming that, either!). She was sure beyond all ambiguity exactly how that profession appeared, and, armed with this immutable information, she rejected any possibility of pursuing anything connected to art. Martha found it difficult even to fantasize about being an artist.

Ways to Change Rigid Thinking

Being in the state of ambiguity enables your imagination to develop options, as it did for Hamlet and Polonius. The following method will help you develop those fantasy skills:

Exercise 8.2: CUTTING UP

a) Cut up pictures from magazine ads into irregular shapes. First look at your shapes without trying to define them. Then give each shape at least three names.

Practice by "seeing" different objects and things in the above shape.

b) Now look at the following picture. What or whom do you see? Focus your eyes on the dot in the middle of the page. (Below we'll have some answers. But don't peek yet!)

In the first example, people have identified such things as a boat, Chinese characters, a person sleeping in a tent with feet hanging out, a waterfall, and part of a rainbow. In the second example, did you see both the old and the young woman? They are both there! What else did you see? Some people have seen a gorilla and an eagle.

You are strengthening your ability to view things kaleidoscopically. That is, you encourage yourself to see patterns in a variety of ways. Even if the item seems obvious, suspend your need to see it that way for the sake of practice.

Assumptions

Assumption comes from the Latin word *sumptus*, to take charge of, to take by choice, and *adsumere*, to take to oneself. Avoid making hasty conclusions about a situation before you give it time to "develop." For example, if the driver ahead of you does something you disapprove of, try to think of creative reasons why. If they drive very slowly, maybe there is a sick parakeet on board, or if they are driving too fast, perhaps they are transferring Contra funds to another account before the authorities catch them. Go on both sides in your mind (not with your car, of course!) before you try to figure things out.

The greatest deterrent to ambiguity is the unconscious use of assumptions in your belief system. Unreflected assumptions slam the door on your storehouse of divergent ideas, and exclude information needed for a more complete picture. Unconscious assumptions (also called prejudice) are sometimes so subtle that they can escape attention. One example from a newspaper headline:

ARABS RELEASE 8 WOMEN AND 5 BLACKS

The assumption? That the women are white and the blacks are male. The norm is white males, who don't require special identification. Language supports a similar assumption that doctors are male unless proved otherwise. If doctors who are female are called women doctors, who are the doctors? (You guessed it.) Is it any wonder that fewer women aspire to be doctors? (The opposite is also true for the word nurse.)

The only occupations restricted as to sex are sperm donor and wet nurse. Unconscious assumptions narrow conclusions, block possibilities, and perpetuate rigid approaches. Don't prematurely restrict your mission dreams to one possibility! The only limitations to your calling are the ones you impose on your own mind.

Ambiguity: Catching Yourself with Your Assumptions Down

To assume anything unconsciously makes an **ass** out of **U** and **me**. Dropping assumptions allows you to "go on both sides" before coming to a conclusion.

You can't suspend something which is not in your consciousness! Being conscious of your assumptions gives you the flexibility and vulnerability to allow for alterations, revisions, and changes. One-way thinking begets only the same. The sequence of the ambiguous process is as follows:

> **starting position** > **conscious suspension of assumptions** > **ambiguity** > **generate options** > **make choices** > **conscious selection of position** > **conscious assumption admitted.**

In a workshop, Eduard de Bono told of a juvenile locked in a local jail who wanted to spend the evening in town, and engineered an elaborate escape by climbing over the walls with sheets used as ropes. Upon his return, the boy discovered the front door was unlocked! He had assumed he needed to break out the hard way.

151

Consciously Getting Rid of Assumptions

Of course, any belief or action has a point of view. The trick is to be consciously aware of your assumption, because it functions like an equation: If I do X, Y will result. And usually those equations tend to be negative, particularly regarding careers. Let's look at what Roger, a young CPA in Westwood by day and a clarinetist by night, came up with:

Roger's Assumptions About Work:

work	= paid activity (usually 8–5 or longer)
paid activity	= pain, drag
pain	= work
play	= whatever I do "off-hours" (music)
off-hours activity	= poor pay
poor pay	= poverty
leaving career	= significant decrease in income
decreased income	= loss of lifestyle
loss of lifestyle	= unhappiness

His conclusion?

work	= pain
play	= poverty
leaving career	= unhappiness

Fulfilling his dreams of performing clearly meant to Roger that he would be poor, unhappy, and leading an unstable life. There was no way out with that kind of rigid thinking. How can Roger find an enjoyable career when he predicts it would mean unhappiness, abandoning a lifestyle, and emotional deprivation?

Roger's other issue was that he was unsure of exactly what his music meant to him and what he wanted to do with it. The CPA job was clear-cut, but without a goal. He was caught in a Catch-22 situation: if he pursued the music, he'd be poor, and if he stayed with the CPA job, it would make him miserable.

Generating Options

Roger had to alter his concept of work. Just for an exercise, I asked him to view it differently than in his usual equations. He was to float with new work ideas (ambiguity), and let them take shape over a period of about two to three weeks. In other words, he was to confront his tendency to make rigid assumptions with premature conclusions. To get ideas, I suggested he look at people he admired, people in professions he liked, or friends, for ideas.

Why are people so envious of football players, TV stars, or comedians? Because they get paid for having fun. A local announcer recently commented on his talk show: "I get paid every day for playing." Roger needed to see that there were people like that in the world.

Not surprisingly, Roger realized that work is not necessarily the painful activity he assumed it to be. Here's what his new work list contained:

Issue: Work Associations

interest
talent
music
joy

physical health
happiness
energy
achievement
fulfillment
satisfaction

The conclusion now? Work (that is music) can bring fulfillment, joy, satisfaction, and good health. Previously Roger had assumed music brought poverty and disappointment. That's why he wanted to give it up. He needed music as a mission. The CPA job was to serve music by keeping Roger financially stable. The path to a healthy point of view began with Roger's willingness to suspend his entrenched thoughts about work and be open to (temporary) ambiguity.

Roger started immediately on his new set of associations with an action plan. He listed anything he could do that very day to get started on the positive road to fulfilling his musical dreams.

Roger's Action Plan:

- List all the ways being a CPA can serve my mission
- List what I enjoy about music
- Find intersection points between them (such as CPA for music company)
- Audition for more gigs
- Investigate a short leave of absence or reduced work time to devote to music
- Enjoy the combination of CPA and musician more!

Roger had changed his assumption from "It's impossible to be happy as a CPA," to understanding that "Being both a CPA and a musician is possible, advantageous and somehow part of my mission." He began

154

to investigate becoming an accountant for freelance musicians, thus moving one step closer to integrating music into his day work. Now Roger's mission has emerged from ambiguity to clarity—reviving the popularity of the clarinet in contemporary pop music.

Exercise 8.3: TAKING ISSUE WITH YOUR ISSUE

Take an assumption which might be holding you back from your mission. Maybe, like Roger, it has to do with combining talents. Follow the exercise through these four stages:

Stage One: GETTING THE ISSUE OUT

*Issue:*_____

My unambiguous (inflexible) assumptions:

_____ = _____

_____ = _____

_____ = _____ *etc.*

Now allow yourself to float with your equations awhile and let your associations become fluid, flexible, fantastic, funny, humorous, silly, even bizarre. Somewhere in all of this the answer you need will emerge. It might take a day or a week, but allow enough time between stages one and two to drift like a cloud.

155

Stage Two: FREE ASSOCIATE:

Issue: _____

Associations:

_____

_____

_____

What changed for you specifically? Examine the areas of difference between stage one and two. What can you do to stay out of the mire of the first? For Roger, it was to reduce his job to four-fifth's time. Make an action plan from your associations. Include one thing you can do *today* to get started.

My Action Plan:

_____

_____

_____

Stage Three: LEARN AND LISTEN ABOUT OTHERS

Read inspirational stories, biographies and auto-biographies of people who have believed in themselves and said yes to their dreams. Success stories help counteract fixed assumptions about what is possible. Betty Ford has survived a mastectomy and drug dependency and built a clinic to help others. Auguste Renoir kept on his artistic mission after his right hand became disabled. After all, if they can do it, you can too!

Mary, Mary, Quite Contrary

For Mary, a young bright woman with an entre-preneurial spirit, red hair and temperament to match, life was completely settled and unambig-uous. For instance, she was fiercely sure that only other people were lucky. She had trouble admit-ting that her life could take any kind of different direction.

Mary once had had big dreams to use her sci-entific skills in the service of children. But how? She "only" had a B.S. in Mathematics. "And be-sides," she thought, "everyone knows you can't make money with children."

Finally, she agreed to float awhile. She went to a local library, and read about Candy Lightner, the woman who founded MADD (Mothers Against Drunk Driving). She saw what one person could do! That article changed her way of making assumptions. Rather than boxing herself in with unambiguous, fixed equations, she remained flex-ible and allowed ideas to come to her (much like Einstein did while shaving).

One result of her new approach is that she has initiated children's projects at a girls' club in which the youngsters can explore and develop an ap-preciation for math, or making scientific displays. (Her window design skills came in handy for this.)

Stage Four: KEEPING THE BABY

Fixed thinking leads many people to get rid of an entire idea once they have rejected it. But that can be like throwing the baby out with the bath water. When you make transitions in your life, there will frequently be a recycling of past experience, knowledge, and skills.

The following exercise will help you determine whether you want to eliminate everything (baby and bath water) or retain some elements (the baby). Your mission will become clearer when you know which components you want to keep.

Here's how this exercise worked for me. I no longer wanted to teach German at the university, and I thought that this meant giving up all forms of teaching.

I found out to my surprise that I wanted to keep some of the elements of teaching:

Bath Water:	*Baby:*
employee status	flexibility
grading papers	speeches
university setting	teaching
meetings	art/culture
committees	flexible schedule
semester system	ideas
grading papers	teaching
German grammar/lit.	counseling
student population only	
lectures	

I wanted to leave the specific environment I had been in, as well as some peripheral aspects: the university setting, meetings, committees, teaching

German, grading papers, being an employee, and the semester system. I wanted to continue teaching, giving speeches, having a flexible schedule, counsel, and travel (for the first time travel was possible in October, and not, as I had assumed, in the summer).

What would the new combination add up to? I took the parts which remained behind, mixed the pieces, adding some new elements, and came up with my new mix:

have my own business
music (composing, singing)
writing
motivational work
lecture on creativity

The "cloud" or "jigsaw pieces" turned into creativity workshops, seminar design, Life Mission counseling, public speaking, and performing. In other words, I recycled what I had done previously, and came out with something new. The sequence:

Issue > Component parts (Baby/Bath Water) > What I wish to keep > New mix > Final picture(s)

Exercise 8.4: SAVING THE BABY

Now do the same, using a career you are struggling with:

159

1) Give the list a title, and jot down all the component parts.
2) Like a smorgasbord, select the items you want to keep and separate them from the ones you want to eliminate.
3) Look at your "baby" and see what these words suggest to you and add anything you want to keep, if applicable.
4) Put each word on a slip of paper and the slips into a hat. Take any three slips and place them side by side. Ask yourself what each combination suggests. Remain open and flexible. Add to this list as much as you like.

Row Your Boat: Flowing with Ambiguity

In ambiguity you suspend certainty in order to find it. The round *"Row, Row, Row Your Boat"* is a metaphor for that paradox.

Row, row, row your boat
Gently down the stream
Merrily, merrily, merrily, merrily,
Life is but a dream.

The river knows which way it is going, it has a sense of purpose. The song invites you to go with the flow— the river's flow. Row down the river GENTLY, following its path, capitalizing on its energy, knowing that it will guide you to your destination. The trip naturally takes shape along the way.

A river has a bed and two banks. Without them, it would be a delta without definition or direction. Ambiguity provides an opportunity to flow and drift within the overall framework of direction. Ambiguity makes life wiggly and interesting. Imagine a straight river— no bends, twists, or oxbows—boring! The same is true of life.

The choice is yours. Look at the clouds and enjoy the show! Ambiguity is your admission ticket.

Chapter Nine

Ideate, Then Incubate

C an you imagine that, instead of saying "Let there be light," God had said, "Golly, I'm stuck. I want to do something, but what?" Without ideas, nothing happens. The same is true of your mission: to realize it you must learn to generate ideas—lots of them.

Ideas are your imaginative thoughts and responses to situations in the moment. They can be an inventive way to prepare an old recipe, putting two things together into something new, taking a piece of piping and a hub cap and making a table out of it, finding a new use for something (like turning an old porcelain sink into a birdbath), or converting those 500 ping-pong balls from an unsuccessful garage sale into sound-proofing for your daughter's percussion room.

Ideas solve problems, stimulate and spark more

162

ideas. They provide the options and freedom to pursue your desired goals. The creative mission seeker (what you're learning to be in this book) must be a veritable idea factory.

This chapter therefore shows you:

1) what ideas are
2) where and how to come up with them
3) how to transform your idea killers into positive action
4) the value of incubation.

The goal is to accurately pinpoint your life mission by generating abundant ideas.

Education and Ideation at Odds

Ideation is nothing new. It simply means the formation of ideas. You've done that ever since childhood. You turned piles of sand into castles, invented interesting creatures to talk to, or fantastic ways to get to the moon. (NASA certainly had nothing on your fantasy—you were going to the moon long before it actually happened). At some point you learned the difference between fantasy and reality and realized you weren't being rewarded for transforming things into something they were "not."

To stay safe or avoid criticism you began to use linear, logical thought patterns and shut down your creativity. The system forced you to abandon your ideational talents. Facts were demanded instead of fantasy. When was the battle of Waterloo (fact), instead of what might have happened to the course of history if Napoleon had won? (fantasy) Why does the color of blue eyes mean something different from brown? Or as I asked once in school, why do people use the word he

163

for everybody when over half of the world's population is female? Why are the words writer, actor, teacher invariably supposed to be male? "It's grammatically correct," replied the teacher, nervously fidgeting with his dress.

Hit 'Em Again, Hit 'Em Again, Harder! Harder! The Idea Killers' School Cheer

Idea killers are phrases or statements which prevent you from considering an option. They have a devastating effect on your ability to pursue your mission. In an exercise, participants tackled a problem by generating ideas. They were unaware of the fact that all groups but one had a negative stooge who was to kill every suggestion proposed.

One group, however, contained a person who greeted each new item with encouragement (without being too obvious—after all, such behavior can arouse suspicion!). The group with the supportive "plant" generated more ideas than all the rest!

Of course, you can perform the same "ideacide" by yourself. Here are some idea killers a writer friend generated:

- No one will read it
- The market is already glutted with similar topics
- I haven't anything new to say
- It will never sell
- I haven't got the talent
- It's not worth the time
- I don't have a publisher
- Who needs it?
- I haven't the expertise to do this

- I can't afford the time away from generating income to write
- I won't earn anything from it

A depressing list! Those phrases can literally knock the energy right out of you. Try surfing or balancing on a beam and then say the words "I can't make it, I'm going to fall." See how long you stay upright!

Daniel, a young professor of sociology, told the story of his student entrance exam for an Eastern college. There was a physical part to the test, consisting of climbing a rope to the ceiling of a room. Daniel had been up rather late the night before, and arrived fairly groggy for the test. Before he realized it, he had climbed up to the top with one hand. As he descended, he was told he had to go back up and touch his nose to the ceiling (part of the requirement), and as he began to think about how impossible this would be, he couldn't perform with two hands the same thing he had done with one a minute before.

All Daniel heard was his inner voice saying "I can't," even after he had just performed that task successfully! Remember, if you say you can or you can't, you're right!

You Can Get Away with Murder (of Idea Killers)

Alright, all you pistol-packing mamas (and papas), here are two ways to blow away your idea killers and get away with it.

1. Activate that child within you. When you were young and dreamed of becoming a sea captain or queen of the universe, your critical self didn't come along and say, "CAMAAAAN, do

165

you really think you're going to do that?" A child's fantasy doesn't include such sophisticated deterrents. Do childlike things—observe how children are free to think in ways you may have forgotten. Allow yourself to daydream as you once did as a child. Play with possibilities. Whenever imagination is valued and taken seriously, your critic doesn't have a chance.

2. Become irrational! When you get what you want, the process never "adds up"! Generating "irrational" ideas is the stuff of which exciting missions are made. The opposite of irrational thinking is the linear way. Things must add up: $2 + 2 = 4$, for example. It expresses things in terms of before and after, cause and effect, right and wrong. There is one solution and a prescribed way to arrive at conclusions. Linear thinking generates old rather than new material. It never shows anything new: $2 + 2 + 2 + 2$ always equals 8.

Exercise 9.1: TRANSFORM YOUR IDEA KILLER LIST.

After making a thorough idea killer list of your own, replace each item with statements as boldly positive as the negative ones you had. The writer replaced "Who needs it?" on the list with: "This book is as important for the world to have as a square meal."

After finishing your idea killer list, destroy it and keep only your positive thoughts. Each time new ones emerge, repeat the process. Post your new statements in a prominent place in your house.

Destroying lists offers no guarantees per se. The value of this exercise is to keep those idea killers out of your consciousness. It's like emptying your closets; there is no guarantee that you'll not go back to cluttering them. But, by the physical act of removing things, you are making a statement: "I only want positive ideas in my mind uncluttered by idea killers."

Practice Makes Perfect

Practice leads to improved performance, whether it be in memorizing, typewriting, piano playing, or ideation. Take piano scales. You might practice them for years, when finally, the payoff comes—you've reached a stage where you can do them automatically. That Bach fugue suddenly becomes a joy because you know how to play your scales.

Likewise, generating ideas comes through practice. Ideation needs practice before it can be automatic. And like scales, ideas are a tool to get you where you want to go.

Exercise 9.2: COOKING ON ALL BURNERS—
YOUR EMOTIONAL WARM SPOT

We'll concentrate on ways to generate and evoke ideas within you. First, ideas need a nourishing environment to bear fruit. An exercise called the *Emotional Warm Spot* (EWS) will show you how to create that space.

167

By EWS, I mean a place in or around your child-hood home where you went to feel safe, where you could be most at one with yourself, where you could be you. It's a location with very special sensory association (seeing, smelling, etc.). Think of these associations as functioning much like soil and nutrients do for plant growth. Arousing those sensorial elements helps prepare the brain for ideation, much like a good set enhances the success of a play. Let's look at how Jack and Frances came to their senses:

Jack O' Lantern

Jack was a 42-year-old mechanical engineer experiencing classic symptoms of job burnout. Much of his problem was environmental. He was a creative man working in an aerospace firm in a busy, wide-open modular office with glaring neon lights. But Jack knew his thinking had become unclear, he felt pressured, and his creativity diminished.

The location of Jack's EWS was his childhood bedroom which he kept like a dark retreat. He loved to hole up there and spend hours by himself reading by a small lamp and dreaming up new things to invent. He remembered the smell of the lamp, especially. Is it any wonder he experienced emotional discomfort with his job?

Jack related that he had rejected the EWS notion almost totally during the workshop. While driving home he argued with me mentally but when he turned into his driveway he suddenly realized the EWS made sense. (Guess what Jack could see from his car.)

Without even knowing it, Jack had sought out the same EWS in his ranch-style adult home. He always went to the den for his best ideas where he enjoyed a combination of darkness, one lamp burning, silence, the hideaway, and the feeling of time out from everything. His wife felt hurt. After he told her about the EWS exercise, she finally understood that Jack needed a retreat which involved silence, the smell of the lamp, the darkness, and a childhood feeling, rather than a refuge to escape from her (which she feared). Jack felt better about his need to withdraw, too.

Taking Time to Smell the Trees

As a child, Frances had spent hours in a tree house perched in an apple grove in her parents' backyard. An active girl, she had climbed every inch of that tree and inspected every blade of grass under it. For ideas, Frances found that she absolutely HAD to go outdoors to a nearby park. Now a nurse manager in a large psychiatric ward, for years she had felt guilty about leaving her windowless office at the hospital to get out and reflect. I told her she was doing precisely the right thing.

I suggested she take time before ideation to smell the grass, feel the tree or even climb it if she felt comfortable doing so.

Lofty Feelings

My EWS was on the third floor of our Tudor-style house, looking out over the lawn and the meadow across the street. To this day, I like lofts for creative work. In college I felt miserable living for a semester in a basement apartment. As a student in Germany I experienced similar uncomfortable feelings in a basement pad, but I did not understand the reason why until years later. I especially liked the feeling of literally being on top of things in my perch away from the emotional storms of life.

Exercise 9.3: EWS, EWS, EWS, I'M IN LOVE WITH EWS, EWS, EWS

Locate your childhood EWS. If you had many homes or an unhappy childhood (many of us did), pick the one whose EWS is strongest or clearest in your mind. Think about feeling safe and at one with yourself Where did you go and what did you do? Were you alone or with someone? Recall any sights, smells, sounds, tastes, and tactile sensations that you can.

EWS: Loft

Environment: perpendicular to window, reading

When: daytime, preferably mornings

Sensory Connectors: big windows, wide view, wood ceilings, bright sunshine, big wood desk, green grass, trees

Now:

1. Write down a minor concern for which you have not found a solution and set it aside.

2. Immediately thereafter, recreate a space or place which most closely approximates your EWS.

Use the space for this exercise. (It's also an ideal place to practice all the other exercises in this book.) You may only be able to approximate this space for now. Be creative! If you can't find an apple tree, another kind of tree will do (or a picture of a tree). If you haven't got a backyard, maybe you can use your balcony, or a courtyard at work.

3. After you have located your EWS, take five minutes a day for the next week in your space, reliving all the sensations and images of your childhood EWS you can.

4. Work on the concern you identified and, finally,

5. Write down ideas for possible solutions each day, and then sort them out to pick one as a solution.

Increasing Your Receptivity to Ideas

Think back to the last creative ideas you have had. When did they occur? Just after taking a shower? After taking a walk? Upon finishing a meditation? Or after a quiet period? Chances are, it was after time of solitude or reflection.

Begin ideation with a quiet period. Turn off everything, especially your thoughts and agenda. For your brain, rest is a battery charge. Your goal is to establish an open, receptive mental and emotional state to foster imaginative thinking.

Edison actually put a sofa into his laboratory so that he could take a half hour nap, after which he felt extraordinarily creative. Mozart received his musical themes in dreams. W. Clement Stone advocates several ten-minute naps during the day to allow intuition to flourish. Some people prepare best by exercise, such as jogging or walking, before they tackle an issue of the day. Pick what works for you.

Eight Ways to Get Ideas

Now that you have set the stage with relaxation and your EWS, use this eight-step program to generate yours ideas more effectively. Your objective is to gain some insight about your mission by triggering new ideas in the form of questions, each of which reflects a different perspective on the issue. It's like turning the kaleidoscope a bit to see a new pattern—ideas will form as soon as you do that. We'll use two basic approaches, 1) asking questions in a new way, and 2) making new associations.

Exercise 9.4. PART ONE: ASKING QUESTIONS WITH "What if . . ."

Select a problem you wish to solve. For now, don't worry about whether it relates to your mission. This is a practice session to increase your ideational skills. Let's say your problem has to do with commuting to work. Pose it as a question, using *What if . . .* as a starting point. The *What if . . .* method will shed light on the real issue and will suggest solutions. How can I solve the problem of driving a long time to work?

1. Change the perspective of the problem. Change *driving > not driving.* What if someone else did the driving? The question could be: What if I stopped driving? What if I took a helicopter to work? What if I hired a chauffeur to drive me? Went in a van pool? And so on. Use the "I" form in asking the questions.

2. Change the focus to another part of the question, by turning it around. I go to work > work comes to me. What if you didn't need to commute at all? What if the job were located where you live? *What if* you took up residence in the organization for which you work? They may wonder about the sofa bed you have in the office, and the late hours. Or *What if* you worked in your own home?

3. Replace part or all of the question with something else. Work > somewhere else. Maybe your commuting question has to do with the place you are going to instead of how much time you need to get there. What if you were going to a golf course for eight hours? To a resort? A park? (Forget for a moment whether you can afford this or not, the point is to get used to seeing the question from different angles.) How does the idea of a longer commute seem now?

4. Exaggerate the question. Sometimes you can change the degree of the question. Change "work" to something else. *What if . . .* you had the most delightful job on earth? Suddenly, that hour or forty-five minutes might not look so bad! If it still looks awful, then you know in part it has to do with the commute.

5. Make your question silly or fanciful. Freeze-dried coffee came about from a water-logged ship loaded with coffee. Then somebody suggested: "What if we froze these soggy coffee beans"? It was decided to save the coffee by freezing it. The

173

solution came from the willingness to consider a crazy question. Don't exclude wild and woolly answers, like bringing the work to you. What if you bought the building in which you work and had it transported to your backyard? You'd certainly eliminate your commute! The question to consider might then be: would I *want* my workplace next door?

Now, if sleeping in your office, plopping huge buildings in your backyard, or flying helicopters seem a bit far-fetched, they are alternatives, albeit somewhat outrageous. Yet, within these alternatives are kernel ideas for solutions.

By turning the problem into various *"What if . . ."* situations (exaggerate it, turn the question around, or make it silly) you highlight many facets to the problem: the workplace, driving location, time, distance, type of work, etc. The list is endless, but I hope these five tips get you started. Each will give you new insight into the problem and an idea for a solution.

Here are possible solutions to the commute problem as suggested by *"What if . . ."*
You could:

- begin working out of your neighbor's home
- get the boss to move the company near you
- eliminate the job
- move to a rural area which requires less commuting
- quit your job (perish the thought!)
- win a lottery ticket and buy out the business
- perform tasks by telephone or computer
- engineer a friendly takeover
- get a wing transplant from an angel

Practice now by choosing a concern of your own, and pick several ways to approach it with "*What if...*" questions. The object is to stimulate new ideas. Allow yourself to be fanciful, creative, humorous, and imaginative.

Make any revisions on the way you stated your concern. What method worked best for you? Review the options you have generated and for now, put your work away.

**my concern > elements > ideas > possible
solutions**

Exercise 9.4. PART TWO: NEW ASSOCIATIONS

A frequent quagmire in ideation is that options and solutions tend to follow the same patterns. Random items give the brain fresh material to work with, associations that help avoid using your logical left brain. You're looking for alternate perspectives to get out of thinking ruts.

The next part gives you further methods to generate ideas, this time using words, objects, and forms as mental triggers to get away from the problem.

6. Open a dictionary to a random page. Pick out a word randomly. Now force-fit that word to your problem. Suppose the word was "rock." How can the word "rock" give you insight about your problem, say driving to work? You might come up with a rocky path or rock music. You may feel that the rat race is making you as hard as a rock and no longer human to the rest of those around you. Or

maybe you should play rock music while commuting. The process:

word > association > force-fit to problem > insight

Objects are heavily laden with remembrances,
such as where they were bought, who was with
you when you bought them, what you were feeling, the person who gave them to you, or what
you were doing at the time. These sensorial elements, as we learned with the EWS, encourage
new ideas. A random object will encourage "illogical" connections.

7. *Take any ordinary object in your immediate vi-
cinity.* List the attributes of this object on a sheet
of paper. What is its size, shape, volume, length,
color(s), texture, material? Select one of the attributes, and see what you free associate with that
attribute. (For example, if you picked "paper clip,"
and selected the attribute "wire," what things
could you associate with that word?). Put the object out of view, and free associate your attribute
("wire") with the question. The object you select
and the word you come up with seem random, but
they are linked, in some way. What you generate
from the object will have a bearing on the problem, as anything you do has a relation to anything
else, however remote it might seem. The sequence
is as follows:

object > attribute > association > insight

Workshop participants, all nurses, wanted to improve their relationships with physicians. How

could they do it? They divided into several groups, each one with a different object. One group received a bottle of body oil. They picked the attribute "oil" and "rub" as their word association. That word produced "rub the wrong way," "lubricate," "there's the rub," and "rub-a-dub-dub, three men in a tub," among others. Then they worked on discovering the connection and decided that the physicians rubbed them the wrong way, which was no surprise. But how to use the rub as part of the solution?

After some discussion, the nurses realized they needed more support—emotional rubbing and stroking. Since the solution is part of the problem, and vice-versa, I suggested that perhaps the physicians wanted recognition—like rubbing and stroking. "How could this be?" they sniffed.

I asked the nurses if they gave the doctors any praise on their work. "Well, no," they admitted, "the physicians don't need that anyway, because they are already convinced of their superiority." I suggested it might improve things if the nurses started rubbing the physicians the right way, too!

Suggestions began to flow: an exercise class together; massaging problems in a team meeting; easing "rusty" communication with the oil of skilled negotiation; a touch of support on the arm, and so on. All of this insight from a simple bottle of body oil! They realized that rubbing the right way goes both ways and can smooth relations.

8. *Change the form of an issue to get new insights about it.* Select the part of the question which lends itself to transformation. For instance, in the commuting example, either "time," "commute," or

"job" can be transformed. You can shorten, elongate, freeze (remember the coffee), squeeze , magnify, minify, turn upside down, or liquefy that part. Pick what you want to work with. Add your own transformations.

Associate the part with the form you selected. For example, let's say you selected "commute" as the part of the question and you decided to change its form and "liquefy" it. You could find ways to travel on waterways, ski, or travel by boat.

To take another example, if "writer's block" is the part (still using "liquefy"), you could take a squirt gun and splash words on a huge sheet of paper or have a good cry before writing.

If you changed the form to electricity (still using "writer's block"), you could communicate in neon lights or make words into electrical pulses. The object is to gain insight, generate creative ideas, but not necessarily to be practical at this point.

Here's the sequence again:

problem > object > association > insight

Terry the Pterodactyl

I used a variation of the last example in a group exercise called "Terry the Pterodactyl." In this process, an object served as trigger for associations and insights about a problem some managers were having at work.

Prior to the exercise the group identified an issue it wanted to address. Somehow the secretaries were not performing in the efficient manner the managers wanted. What was the reason for this lack of productivity?

I passed out some chunks of clay to each person.

Each participant was to mould the clay into anything they wanted. As the pieces of clay began to take shape, I started a fairy tale, using one participant's object as a point of departure. The object looked like a prehistoric Pterodactyl, whom I dubbed Terry. Terry, I began the story (no sex specified,) was a secretary at this organization and wanted to fly far away.

Then the participants took over and continued the tale, using their object as trigger for the fairy tale plot. Then each person passed their object, together with the growing collage of their predecessors, and their own addition to the fairy tale, on to the next person.

The emerging story was about a female secretary who felt oppressed and burdened by lack of direction from her boss. She never wanted to return because she was never able to do anything right and life had become unbearable and frustrating at work. Terry was an overworked person who was thought of as brainless. It was a no-win situation. Tahiti was just the place where she could escape the complexity and confusion of the office.

In the discussion afterward, questions emerged. Why did Terry want to fly away? Why did she have half a brain? Why was management giving poor leadership? The managers recognized that they were contributing to productivity problems by sabotaging their own secretaries. The method was simple: give unclear directions, expect fast, perfect work, but assume the secretary didn't have the intelligence to complete it, a sure way to reinforce feelings of their superiority (why can't she ever get it right?).

The managers were stunned by what they learned. Rather than coming up with a method to "get those secretaries in line" they had discovered their own complicity in the problem. Changing the form of the tale allowed them to avoid objective, hence threatening, references to "real" people. The solution to their management problems? Clarify objectives, communicate

179

tasks and results more clearly to their secretaries and above all be more supportive. (Most of these men were Doers who were used to getting results but not giving emotional encouragement, as discussed in Chapter 3.)

Creative Connections to Your Mission

Discoveries often occur in an unintended or accidental way when you link things together "randomly." Remember, anything can be connected to anything else. Mr. Birdseye made an expedition and ended up marketing frozen fish by asking a simple "*What If . . .*" question.

On an expedition in the Arctic, Birdseye saw a fish frozen in the ice. He wondered if he could do the same with vegetables and package it for the general public. He took one object (frozen fish) and connected it to another (vegetables) and asked, "What if I froze vegetables and sold them in stores?"

Take out the sheet of paper and write down your question. Now brainstorm some possible "*What If . . .*" ideas. Don't exclude anything. Elimination comes later. Were you able to add to the list? What new ideas did this method generate? Now for the most important question of all. How does your question relate to your Mission? (For Mr. Birdseye, it no doubt had to do with exploration, risk-taking, adventure, and perhaps even convenience.)

What one thing can you do today to work on the issue you selected?

Help! I've Got (Too Many) Ideas!

Some people (usually Motivators) actually bubble over with ideas. Like a flood, they spill over the river's banks without shape and direction, turning it into a delta.

Glen the Generator

Glen, a creative free-lance photographer had about as many ideas for missions as there are rides at Disneyland. Since he had received a healthy inheritance from a rich aunt, he felt for a long time that he didn't need to make a choice. He sensed the lack of a mission in his life, grew restless and impatient, flitting about from one idea to the other. But he realized that a mission cannot be ignored.

His task was to decide which choice was best for him in any given situation. I asked him to list those careers he was most attracted to emotionally. He produced a computer print-out of over one hundred! Then he prioritized them on a scale of 1–10, coming up with twenty-five. He was reluctant to "reduce" his options for fear he would have to give up the others. Glen wanted to have it all, but having what he wanted was having it all!

Glen's problem was that he was not aware of what he wanted. Giving himself permission to go for something he liked specifically seemed selfish, like an ego-trip. His inability to decide was like craving some kind of food without knowing what. Relief comes only in identifying precisely what it is. When you find it, the craving also stops. But Glen had been told what to like or dislike his entire life. His own agenda had become clouded and buried. Glen didn't believe he had the right to have specific, focused desires and that's why he proliferated options.

Glen recognized that he wanted to write screenplays. He had bought a computer and was passionately in love with it. Up to then, he had used it solely for correspondence! Part of him had already figured out he wanted to be a writer. A mission was realized as the writer began to make pictures with words.

He took a week to clear out his apartment (Motivators like Glen tend to gather clutter). He gave away

$1500 in books, did some more clearing out of clothes and furniture (incubation!), sat down and wrote out ideas for a screen play, and then finished it in one week. He now has an agent and is busy looking for a producer for his play.

Incubation: Putting Ideas on Hold

Part of any creative process is incubation. As any farmer knows, there is a period after planting seeds when you give them time to sprout and blossom according to a plan which has its own rules and timing. Mission ideas need to incubate, too. Witness the cicada which takes seventeen years to grow into its adult form. Those people who have difficulty with incubation often find themselves leaping before they look, rushing from one solution to another without allowing anything to come to fruition. They deny the natural growth and development of their mission.

Incubation of ideas need not necessarily last months (as Analyzers think). Sometimes incubation can be a matter of seconds (Doers like that). It might involve doing some deep breathing before handling the crisis, or periodically getting up for brief stretches before returning to the word processor, or pacing around the room before making a decision.

Practice putting your ideas to rest for awhile! Alan Lakein tells of advising a disorganized client to take a weekend trip to think things over. The client gained immensely from his quietude. Jesus went out to the desert for forty days. Many people I know play eighteen holes of golf. Other methods include meditation, visualization, sleep, dreams, exercise, breathing, guided imagery, playing music, doing "right brain" (non-verbal) exercises, or removing yourself from the company of others. Many people already know about "sleeping on things," yet during the hectic day they can't or won't take time for reflection and solitude. There is a temptation for immediate action, to pounce upon ideas and implement them without taking time to let them percolate. It's like cooking your grandma's favorite stew in ten minutes. Moreover, this is an age of instant gratification, of having what you want when you want it. You've been conditioned to the end result, in contrast to the importance of letting ideas ripen in the process. Ideas require patience—and germination time.

Incubation and Your PM

If you are a Doer type, you especially need to sleep on your ideas. They may seem wonderful and ready for implementation, but a day or two later, they will probably be better (when you wait an extra day for the tomato to ripen, it tastes more delicious). Motivators need time for focusing and clarification of choices. Stabilizers will be comfortable with incubation, perhaps too comfortable, since they can slowly arrive at the most logical conclusion. Analyzers will need to stop gathering information. They need to stop, incubate, and then make a decision without succumbing to the temptation to remain indecisive.

The Value of Logic in Ideation

Successful people are those who know how to balance creative ideas, risk-taking, spontaneity, and incubation with their logical, critical side. After incubation, you

183

Finding Your Life Mission

can use logic as a check and balance. Think of logic as your safety net. It's there to check any slip or fall but does not interfere with the creative high wire act.

Logic can also save you time. If you're busily cutting the lawn with a pair of scissors, it might be creative for whatever reason, but not terribly pragmatic. (Unless you are doing it at midnight, and there is a ban against mowing at that time.) Logic is especially applicable when the problem has only one good solution.

Motivators will resist logic the most. They have been known to do crazy things, like driving from Los Angeles to Las Vegas via Utah. Analyzers, on the other hand, are prone to be logical and rule oriented. Remember, it was undoubtedly Analyzer types who pleaded with NASA officials (Doers) not to send up the Challenger because they knew that it was dangerous!

Ideas for Your Life Mission

Make a general statement about your Life Mission concern now. Let's say it's "My mission is to make people see the funny side of life," or "My mission is to make order out of chaos," or, "My mission is to live closer to nature." Turn the statement into a question. For example, "What if I bought a house in the country?" Use any of the above seven methods that appeal to you. Open the dictionary and get a word which you link to that mission.

Think of your Life Mission as clay to be shaped by you. List any options, draw a line underneath the last one and put the paper away. That's called incubation.

Return to your Life Mission only when you have given it enough time for your creative and your logical side to mull your ideas over. It might be a matter of days, but it could be weeks or even longer. When the time is right, you will know which one to pursue.

If you are already bursting with ideas, and have chosen your best, now what? An idea is only useful if you follow it through. Before it becomes a reality, you need to feel it in every fiber of your body and test it in the laboratory of your mind.

Before setting out on a mission, you must first journey within.

Chapter Ten

Visualize Solutions

I never saw a moor,
I never saw the sea;
Yet know I how the heather looks
And what a wave must be.

—EMILY DICKINSON

"See" comes from the Sanskrit word *veda*, which means knowledge, particularly sacred knowledge. Vision gives the mental and spiritual blueprint to manifest desires. Visualization has little to do with the physical ability of sight. Instead, it's a process of seeing your needs on an interior level.

If the light in your tunnel has gone out because you are blocked from seeing your mission, this chapter will help you rekindle the flame of what you desire, manifest that vision, give it resonance to expand outward into your consciousness, and fine tune it to what you want. Finally, we'll discuss a form of visualization called guided imagery and learn how to interpret the seemingly random information it supplies for your mission.

186

Neglecting your visual resource is like overlooking the available parking spaces at the far end of a shopping center lot. It seems to take longer to get where you want, but in the end, it's easier and with far less hassle. Visualization might seem to be some sort of hocus-pocus or underhanded method like insider trading, because you don't have to "do" anything. But it does require inner work: persistence, patience, faith, discipline, focus, and the willingness to give up control—qualities I have discussed many times in this book.

Visualization is what the Rainmaker, in Robert Johnson's story of the same name, calls "getting right inside myself first." In this story, townspeople in India thought that the rainmaker, whom they had asked to come and end their drought, had caused it to rain, when in fact he was only preparing for four days in his hut by "getting right inside [himself]."

Internal work, of which visualization is a part, is much the same as that rainmaker's preparation. "Making it rain," that is, manifesting your desire, always begins with the vision of what you want and comes from tuning in every bit as much as from actual action.

Everything comes in due season and proceeds according to plan. If you simply sit down and put a Mercedes, a mansion, or a yacht into your visual hopper of desire, then look at your watch and expect them to appear in five minutes, you're going to be disappointed. Leave the production and final say to your Source while going about your business. Like the townspeople, thank your Source (= rainmaker) when you get your wishes granted.

Visualization is paradoxical: You visualize what you need based on what you want, and then wait for divine guidance to obtain the perfect solution at the perfect time. And, if you don't get what you hoped to, then affirm: "If not this, then something much better." You'll always get what you need that way!

Seeing by the Sea

When I moved to San Francisco, I was going through a difficult career transition. I made the decision to resign from a tenured university position in favor of an uncertain future. I thought that nothing was materializing in S.F. My vision for the future was temporarily blocked, a sure sign that I was not in the right place (I learned that later). I decided to move to Southern California.

A major concern was the air quality. I knew Santa Monica had the best air, but apartments near the ocean are hard to get. People had told me horror stories of looking there for a year and giving up. But, I had clear visions of the apartment and even the street where it was located. I made a random call to a local Women's Center and asked if the director knew of any apartments in Santa Monica. "No," she replied, "but I do have the name of a woman whom I had contacted three years ago. She manages a lot of apartments; perhaps she might know of something."

A large apartment, exactly what I had envisioned, was available: high cathedral ceilings, balconies, a loft, security parking, and in the precise location where I had visualized it. Too good not to be true! I told the manager it was a miracle such a beautiful apartment was available. She smiled and said: "Well, I guess this apartment was meant for you." But how to pay for the rent? I moved in anyway. A week later, my sister phoned to say she was moving to California, and needed a place to stay. She shared the expenses for ten months, which was just what I needed to get on my feet financially, and it helped her, too.

Learning How to Visualize

Senses help the brain connect to memory and emotion. You can encourage your ability to recall an entire past experience, and for our purposes here, the visual aspects of that experience, by using the sensorial associations of sound, taste, smell, sight, and touch as triggers.

You probably have had the experience of seeing something and remembering the sound or smell attached to it. Maybe on a trip to your old hometown you visited your grade school and could actually recall your teacher's voice resounding through the halls. Perhaps the smell of clover reminds you of summer vacations. These sensory associations are also linked to emotions. That smell of clover can jog your memory of the happiness you felt in summertime at your Aunt and Uncle's farm.

There was once an ad on the freeway that boasted, "See Palms Springs for Half the Bread." A half loaf of bread, hot and steaming, was visible in the background. The ad was effective not only because it appealed to creativity, but also because it conjured up all the associations with bread that make a vacation attractive: nurturing, food, home cooking, grandma. The ad makers knew that people draw on these associations and capitalized on that fact cleverly.

Eye Openers

We'll examine visualization from two perspectives: 1) the ability to give yourself emotional permission to

189

visualize just what you desire, and 2) the technical ability of visualizing your dream job or a delicious vacation spot in your mind. For example, David Karr, a famous doublebass player, was asked how he would describe the sound of the doublebass. Karr, a passionate lover of his instrument, replied without hesitation: "Like chocolate—sweet, smooth, creamy, and dark."

Desire is a word people use gingerly. It is often linked to sexual or primordial urges. But desire is actually a fundamental and intense longing which literally means "to regret the absence of something." You must be able to visualize what you truly desire. By using and encouraging your senses, you strengthen your desires by giving them dimension and substance. Coaxing your desire through the senses is a primary aspect of visualization.

Exercise 10.1: COMING TO YOUR SENSES

The next exercise will take you through various sensory stages, supplying you with the emotional needs for your mission from a sensorial point of view. Do this with a friend or use a cassette tape so that you can go through it without interruption.

- Imagine the taste of your favorite food as a child. Describe the experience surrounding this food (peeling tangerines under the Christmas tree, for example) and then recall the taste of the food.
- Imagine the feel of a favorite pet from childhood. Describe the animal and then see yourself petting it.

Follow the same procedure for the subsequent examples:

- Imagine the smell of early morning after a rain.
- Imagine the sound of children playing on a distant playground.
- Recall your first childhood friend, then see her or him.
- Add some of your favorite sensory remembrances to this list.
- Go for a walk in the morning and concentrate on one sense each morning. Concentrate on taking your walk with only that sense in operation. What kinds of things did you notice that were different? How much more did you hear, see, smell, etc., on the day you devoted to that particular sense? Which one did you respond to most vividly?
- Now observe how you describe or remember things. Did you talk about a recent vacation in terms of what you saw, or the quiet you experienced, or how the food tasted?
- Which sense seems to be dominant?
- After these preparations, list on a sheet of paper the way you want your mission to feel, touch, taste, look, and smell. Be specific. If you want it to be sweet, that isn't enough. You have to link it to something focused, like Lily-of-the-Valley, or burning autumn leaves, or apple pies cooling on the windowsill. One person's sweet may be another's saccharine. Your specific associations give your Source personal and specific information.
- Finally, take your dominant sense and work on your associations with that sense, linking them to your mission.

Paul's Cathedral

Paul, a prep school art teacher, had always loved art, but he was frustrated at not making more personal use of it. And his concern about supporting a family was telling him to abandon art altogether for something more "practical," like administrative or corporate work. After working on his sensorial associations, he was able to generate some very specific information about his mission.

Paul identified his dominant sense as smell. He had been unaware of that preference, and during our work, discovered a poem he had written in high school which had almost entirely used olfactory descriptions.

Paul then related how his mission smelled of scented cathedrals. Having grown up in France, he would wander as a boy through candle-lit cathedrals. He recalled especially the smell of incense just after mass.

Scented cathedrals, Paul discovered, explained his love of art. But he knew that already. I asked him to pick an additional association between smell and mission. He came up with clean sheets! Suddenly a personal childhood experience in a hospital gave the clue: he associated clean sheets with medical care!

He knew now that somehow, that in the combination of medical care and art lay the clue to his mission— but what? He went through several possibilities linking the two. After meditative thought, he felt his preferences had more to do with indirect care through art than teaching (which was what he had been doing previously). Paul came up with the following possibilities:

- create toys for doctor's offices
- become an art therapist
- manage an art therapy program at a hospital
- organize art events for patients recovering from illness
- write about the use of art in recovery

192

- conduct art seminars for health care professionals.
- design interiors for hospitals

Now Paul was focused and ready to attract an answer. Soon after, two opportunities (= answers) arose. One, a position in a children's hospital and the other as a marketing director for a hospital. One building was a spanking clean new building, the other an older (somewhat scented and musty) religious institution. Coincidence? Paul took the hospital marketing job.

As Paul's example shows, associations with your senses can give you clues for a mission and career. These associations are personal design elements which set the stage for your own script. For example, the combination of children and art for one person might result in their becoming a lobbyist for art education in a state legislature, or for another person that might translate into being a child therapist or a cartoonist. *Your mix based on your associations* gives you the palette you need to understand your passions and your career needs.

Even if you had the same sensorial associations as Paul's clean sheets, the connections you make are unique to you. Clean sheets might mean travel, family unity, crickets chirping at night, or a host of other clues.

Paul's work required time for reflection. As I have emphasized again and again, your higher source will guide and help you if you have done the spade work, if you are specific as to your needs. You can't fulfill fuzzy goals. If you visualize your need as the Mojave desert, you'll know you've achieved that goal when you are there. But if you visualize yourself "being happy" how will you know when you've gotten what you want?

The more specific you are, the easier it is to manifest your visions! What does being happy mean in concrete terms? Your higher source will forge what you need.

193

Be specific enough, yet non-controlling of the outcome so your mission desire can appear on its own terms. Be sure to clearly state what you want! If you tell a caterer to "make any old thing" for a party you may end up with trayloads of turkey for the annual vegetarian Thanksgiving dinner.

To summarize:

1. Encourage your sensory faculties by practicing on your earlier memories.
2. Sharpen your senses with daily work focusing on one sense.
3. Pick your dominant sense.
4. Pick the top one or two associations and what they suggest to you. This is body work of the deepest (and most profound) order!
5. Connect the associations to something specific.
6. Relate this object to a desire.
7. Find possible expressions of missions suggested by this desire.

A final point. Most goal-setting exercises stop at identifying the goal. I think it helps to visualize the goal beyond the goal. If you want to win a prize, that's fine, but you must also see yourself doing something with the award money and specify that, too. That's wanting the tree to bear fruit, seeing the fruit, and eating it. You must have your cake and eat it, too!

Often, clients tell me they have trouble fantasizing because they fear it might mean they will have to follow through on their desires. They tell themselves that fantasies are unrealistic, a waste of time, something only kids would do (idea killers in essence). They'll do anything to prevent accessing their mission! They are blocked and refuse to let their mission in.

Goethe said once that what you dream and imagine you can do, you can fulfill. In other words, you must first be able to imagine something before you can manifest it.

Exercise 10.2: *SHARPENING VISUALIZATION TECHNIQUES*

Here are some techniques which will help stimulate your ability to visualize. In the following series of short scenes, spend as long as you need until you are satisfied you have gotten a specific image or are feeling connected with the suggestion. Avoid forcing anything. Instead, allow your inner eye to open up. Give this exercise time and avoid judging yourself on how fast you see something.

Today: Recall what you had for breakfast. Be as specific as you can. What did the things you ate taste like? Include the color or feel of the plate, the shape of the cup, the table, chair. Add any smells or sounds if that helps. (Did your cat meow during breakfast, did the phone ring or your child cry?)

Yesterday: Focus on an event from yesterday and see yourself recreating this event. If you were upset, bring that feeling up again. Or, if you talked to someone recollect the sound of their voice, any colors, or temperature. Include anything which helps you make the situation vivid.

Recent Past: Go back to a recent incident— maybe it was an award you received or a festive

195

occasion you attended. Remember as many of the details as you can in your mind's eye.

Tomorrow: Now visualize a familiar place you're going to tomorrow and imagine how it looks, sounds, or smells. Be specific.

Future: Visualize a place you haven't yet seen but would like to visit—maybe someplace you would like to go on vacation. See yourself in the setting, what you are wearing, and what you will be doing. Take along some special objects from your immediate surroundings.

Fantasy: Create something which does not yet exist, perhaps a dream house, a baby not yet born, how you will look in ten years, or your first book. Draw a picture of it, or describe it in a journal in great detail. Include as much sensory detail as possible.

Exercise 10. 3: OPEN MY EYES AND I SHALL SEE . . .

Another way to get around any blocked visions is to use guided imagery. Have a friend read the following guided imagery or record it on tape for playback during the visualization. Use anything you hear as suggestions for what to see. Remember, nothing is at stake here: it is purely an exercise. This is a process so think of it as NO BIG DEAL for now.

Prior to any guided imagery:

1. Sit comfortably with back erect and legs uncrossed on the floor.
2. Take deep breaths to center yourself and prepare for the quieting effects of the imagery. (Doers and Motivators need to spend longer getting centered.)
3. When your breathing has become calm, steady, and deep, begin your visualization.
4. When a suggestion comes to you, go with it and do not analyze it. If you find yourself straying from the original direction, it's okay because there is no right or wrong. (You Analyzers will struggle with this a bit more.) Go with the flow, and neither chase an image away nor block inviting it in.

Exercise 10.4: GUIDED IMAGERY: "MY FANTASY MISSION DAY"

Begin by closing your eyes and focusing on your breath until it becomes steady and even. Let your breath come in and leave your body easily and calmly. Feel your chest and diaphragm moving.

Now imagine that you are about five years in the future, waking up on a fantasy mission day. Get up and walk slowly over to the window of your bedroom. Take a moment to look out the window and see what there is to see. Then walk over to the bedroom door and down the stairs. Pause in the landing to look at the old grandfather clock and note the time before continuing downstairs.

You now head for the front door to fetch the newspaper because today it contains an article about you. You get the paper, go to your breakfast area, and open the newspaper to the section in

197

which your article appears. (PAUSE) Notice how you feel when you do this. Look at the article and make note of its title. Then look at the photograph of you which is accompanying the article. How are you dressed? What is the expression on your face? Are you sitting or standing? Alone or with people? Take time now to scan the article, and observe your reactions to it. What is the tone of the article? What does it say about you? What insights did you get about your mission?

When you have finished, take a pad of paper and a pencil lying nearby, and write down on the pad the first word that describes your emotional response to the article. Draw a line beneath that word and write down three things you are going to do today in connection with your mission. When you have finished, bring back your note pad and return to your present space. Open your eyes when you're back.

Here are some guidelines to help you interpret what you saw. Remember, everything you saw came from you so everything is a personal message. There is no right or wrong, only things you observed.

1. Where did you find yourself resisting the suggestions or having trouble with forming a picture? At what point did that occur?
2. What did you see from the bedroom window?
3. What time was it when you passed the grandfather clock?
4. Did you feel relaxed, rushed, or stressed? How were you dressed?
5. In what section did your article appear in the newspaper?
6. What was the title and the content of the article?

7. Describe your picture accompanying the article.
8. How did you respond to the article emotionally?
9. Discuss the words on your list and what they suggest about your desires and mission.
10. Make any additional observations of your own.

"My Fantasy Work Day" addresses such questions as: What setting would I like to be in? What do I want to be recognized for (newspaper article)? How would I like my day to be structured? Where do I want to live? How am I most comfortable? What does all this reveal about my mission?

Although you might know the gist of it, you may have had trouble seeing the article clearly. You may even resist being in the paper. No matter. You may believe that your visual response is either fantastic or irrelevant. But you can be sure that your Source is providing you a wealth of information. Don't discount it.

Some people are astonished to find that they are not rushing out in a business suit to hit the freeways, or that the newspaper article portrayed them as someone very different than they otherwise would have permitted themselves. One client of mine saw herself as having given a grand benefit for retarded children, raising more than $200,000. She was elegantly dressed and seemed perfectly at ease in that attire.

Joe Goes Home

It was the first time Joe, an insurance salesman, had ever worked on guided imagery. He was surprised that he saw himself staying home. Home? He had been working for ten years outside the home. He had always

199

felt he really needed a place to escape to, an office, since he felt being at home all the time would drive him crazy. Joe realized that he wanted to be home for other reasons than self-employment. But what? The fuzzy cloud slowly took became clear. Part of his mission was to provide a more supportive environment for his kids, to participate in their growth and development, to be a caretaker, qualities which he had always used in his business. The combination of office and home began to make sense to him, and it had crystallized in the visualization.

Visualizations: Making Things Compute

A visualization stimulates apparently "irrelevant" information from within. Did you know that by age thirty you have inside of you the equivalent of over 20,000 volumes of information? Much of this knowledge is not immediately available because you have stashed it away. The things you need to forget are generally discarded. And that's just as well. If you remembered everything, you'd go crazy. So your interior mechanism stores material for selective retrieval. From time to time, when you need enlightenment, data is presented to you from you for interpretation. Your inner wise Source is saying "Here are some things for you to reflect upon."

Let's say you're taking a walk, thinking about a problem in your life, and seemingly random words pop into your head. You might, for instance, dismiss words such as "shrimp," "tables," and "bank accounts," as coincidental items, perhaps because you couldn't immediately find meaning in the combinations. Nothing is accidental, however. Whatever you conjure up is information you need to process. Try those three words

200

right now as an exercise. What do they have in common? The good news is, you already *know* what that internal information means. (There is no bad news! See Chapter Six). In other words, you are the co-creator of your world. If certain words or images occur to you, whether as a result of guidance or "out of nowhere," they do so for a reason.

The objective of visualizations is that you can call up specific information on a particular subject. At first, the information might seem disconnected. But everything your Source provides computes. Any manifestation has meaning, it's just up to you to find out what it is. Disconnected or "unrelated" images, words, feelings, associations, such as occur in visualizations, have been preselected from our vast interior storehouse of knowledge to give insight on your mission. We'll call those "disconnected" items *approximately relevant*.

In the same way, you can link together random things which appeared to you in the visualization. They all make sense, since you put them there. What relation do they have to each other? Do not pay attention to whether your conclusions seem right or wrong.

Trust that an offering from within is given to you as a gift. Receive it gratefully and unwrap it. You only know what it is when you uncover it. Treat each visualization as an opportunity to access your internal computer. You have so much wisdom to draw upon! By using your intuition, you process the wisdom within faster than any computer. You'll learn to trust it as a loving guide, confidante, lover, and sage.

In the next chapter, we'll visit this special friend. Mission wanted: inquire within.

Chapter Eleven

Inquire Within

Nach innen geht der Weg. *(The way goes within.)*

—HERMANN HESSE

"So if you don't know it, know it!" I heard thundering from the house next door to us at our vacation spot in Florida. Those were true words of wisdom that accompanied hurled plates smashing against the kitchen wall. As the angry neighbor recognized, each person has a mandate to find the truth. There is no excuse for ignorance, for not knowing.

Well, how do you learn to know what you know? Inquire within (= IW). You are the source of your knowledge. It's an *inside* job. So if you don't know it, know it!

The Inner Quest: Your Real I.Q.

An inner quest requires a kind of isolation, a willingness to exclude everything and deal with yourself honestly and fairly. It's a journey made just by you alone, in order to consult with your internal guides. IW means you are taking a radical turn from working on others' agendas to following your own desires. This inner quest is the I.Q. worth having.

You Doers and Motivators must remember that inner work requires patience. It's not like instant coffee. A client called me several days ago and told me she finally figured out an exercise that I had given her over two years previously! Stabilizers will need the courage to trust their own voice, and Analyzers will need to shut off their rational, critical voice.

The goal of this chapter is to demonstrate that 1) the answers to your search are within; 2) IW requires a shift in focus from outward to inward; 3) you must consult with yourself to the *absolute exclusion* of external influences and 4) inner work requires total self-honesty. Finally, we'll discuss ways to tap that inner wisdom to realize your quest.

Turning On Your Inner Light

Your inner wisdom contains the seed to fruition within you much the same as a mustard seed contains the blueprint of an entire plant. When you nurture your own seed of wisdom, it will seek the light above, just as a planted seed grows towards sunlight.

Your interior self is filled with marvelous information. Once you begin tapping into that source, your fantasy and imagination will blossom and your mission will rise to the surface. Look at the example of Geri.

Being Wary of Geri

Geri had great difficulty knowing exactly what her mission was. I asked her to tell me when she felt most alive and excited. Her face suddenly brightened as she told me of a vacation she had taken to Ireland, and the thrill she had experienced "seeing all those old buildings and the lovely green of the countryside." A bit o' the wisdom had emerged! How would she like to spend 2–3 months combing through Ireland? "No way," she said, "I can't leave my husband."

Geri had always been wary of listening to herself, but she agreed to try. After several weeks of intense inner inquiry, it became clear that she was really longing for preservation and greenery, for luxurious surroundings and peace. She discovered she felt most at home on campuses and botanical gardens because of the feeling of contentment they evoked in her body.

Suddenly, she sensed her love of plants awakening. She had always tended to them with great love and affection, and friends often asked her to care for their plants while they were on vacation. Her mission was to create beautiful and uplifting environments. She happened to live in a lush part of L.A. Geri had tapped a love and a location right around her where she could explore her mission.

Geri resisted her mission at first since she thought her husband would be adversely affected. She had neatly boxed herself in, telling herself that her desire would dramatically impact other aspects of her life. But, she also realized that she would be unhappy forever if she refused to change herself. Her fulfillment began with a commitment and response to an inner resonance.

Your path might lie buried deep within, yet you get constant clues about it. Unlocking the door within opens the truth about yourself—and compels action.

It unlocks the desire within you which is always there, which is to *express the very mission you are equipped to carry out.*

IW Requires a Shift in Focus from Outward to Inward

IW demands surrender to your mind, body, and spirit. To make this shift within, you must tune out the voices of authority, friends, loved ones, or family. Remember, people are always willing to share a piece of their mind. And it's easy to make suggestions if people don't have to act upon what they suggest.

A verse from the Bible says: "Don't let the world around you squeeze you into its own mold." You are the potter, creator, and shaper of yourself. Your inner self is the repository of your knowledge. As the jazz lyric reminds us: "Only you can tell how deep the well. The well is your soul."

Dutiful Dale

A gentle, caring individual, Dale had lived his life for others. His family had grown accustomed to an affluent lifestyle, but he felt helpless because he couldn't meet his own needs. A right-brained visionary, he had worked for more than ten years in a structured left-brain environment. He had imprisoned himself in a corporate legal department which demanded long hours of tedious fact-finding and research. On the weekends, Dale would literally head for the hills to spend all his available time outdoors, only to return to his dungeon during the week. You could say he was paid dearly—or paid dearly—for his trouble.

Dale used his family's demands for an affluent lifestyle as an excuse to avoid dealing with his own issues.

205

I encouraged him to go within and look at his problems independently of anyone else. After visiting a monastery retreat where he spent three days consulting with himself, Dale came to an important insight. He realized he had lied to himself for many years by telling himself he had to maintain his family's expectations while denying his own need for creativity and freedom.

He decided to keep his city job for another year or so, while exploring a law practice in a rural community near the mountains, where he could enjoy a practice as a small-town lawyer/environmental advocate and be on a more personal basis with his clients. Now meditation and inner dialogue are a regular part of his life. His family resisted at first, but when they saw the change in Dale's mood, they gradually accepted his needs. (And, they got more in touch with their own, since Dale wasn't holding up the sky for them anymore.)

The Mach 1 Experience

If you knock on your inner door, open it a crack, get scared, and slam it shut at first, it's all right! But do it! It will strengthen your resolve to open up more the next time. You validate yourself every time you decide to turn to yourself for answers.

The going gets rough as you approach the threshold of truth. You might be willing to trust yourself on low risk questions, but for the biggies, such as "What is my soul's path?" "How can I accept the artist, negotiator, business executive, neighborhood activist, or beekeeper in me?" or "How can I juggle all this with the mortgage payments?", if you need to resort to logic and reason, you'll find those two "friends" usually put the "kibosh" on any internal desires.

In the movie *The Right Stuff*, there was a scene about breaking the sound barrier. Just before the pilot, Chuck Yeager, went through Mach 1 (the speed of sound), the plane shuddered, shook, and resisted. We didn't know if it would make it. Suddenly, the plane soared into serene, glorious, thrilling silence. No more resistance or difficulty, just a peaceful smooth ride.

I call that the **Mach 1 Experience**. The willingness to go through the perturbations of Mach 1 made the rest easy. If you go up to a certain point and then say, "This is too painful; I don't want to deal with it," you keep that barrier before you. There is no better way to break through your Life Mission resistance than go through it! Allow yourself to be "shaken up" so you'll get to experience the smooth ride of your calling.

Here's another way to look at it. Larry Dossey, in his book *Space, Time & Medicine* (Shambhala, 1982) discusses a shaking-up process in nature first identified by Ilya Priogogine in his Theory of Dissipative Structures. (It won Priogogine a Nobel prize.)

Priogogine's ideas have to do with molecular structures in nature. Those structures which evolve into greater complexity, i.e., escape to a higher order, acquire the quality of fragility, the capacity for being shaken up, which paradoxically is also the key to growth. "Structures that are insulated from disturbance are protected from change. They are stagnant and never evolve toward a more complex form," Dossey notes.

Do Disturb

Applying Priogogine's theory to the human condition, if you want to grow, change, and evolve toward your mission, you must be vulnerable to disturbance, especially if you are a complex being (which you are).

Of course, if you opt for being a simpleton, for the mundane and the safe, this process isn't for you. Without the willingness to be "perturbed," there is no complexity and no chance for growth.

Avoiding the Mach 1 Experience protects you from experiencing disturbance but blocks movement towards change. Absence of movement means stagnation and death. Evolving demands that you let yourself be shaken up. Avoiding your inner wisdom is dangerous, because then you remain the same, as Priogogine's theory shows. The going can get rough as you approach the threshold of truth, but the reward is smooth sailing.

Dossey quotes from F. Barron's studies of creative individuals in which he found that they are comfortable with complexity and disorder, the irrational, the magical, the primitive, the nonsensical. "The truly creative individual stands ready to abandon old classifications and to acknowledge that life, particularly his [sic] own unique life, is rich with new possibilities."

The payoff for trusting your inner wisdom is enormous because you are investing in yourself! Trust the melody within you and dare to be "irrational."

A Personal Mach 1 Experience: Pam Faces the Music Within

Pam, a V. P. of a large institution, was clearly no longer able to function in the well-paying job she "enjoyed." Her lower back was giving her enormous pain (she was putting too much stress on it by pursuing the wrong mission). Her creativity was at an ebb. Yet she wanted to hang in there until she could retire and sail around the world with her husband. I said if she continued in this manner, there might not be any retirement benefits or world cruise. But Pam clung to this destructive job for two more months, as I worked with her to break through her resistance.

Pam finally agreed to the thing she had dreaded most—leaving a position she knew well and in which she had "made it." Her fears about quitting were enormous. She had to face herself. Who was she without that title? Where would she go now and who would pay the bills?

But, as she allowed herself to be shaken up by leaving, her creativity slowly reemerged and her health improved. She rediscovered latent capacities in herself, one of which was singing! The payoff was renewed health, vitality, and energy whereas she had thought it would be the end of her identity. Now Pam is truly enjoying the same work she was doing, without the stress of her old job and nearer home. This gives her time to devote her energies to her reawakened hobbies. She has put the music back in her life, improved her health, and gotten more in touch with her mission to be a powerful organizational leader.

Consulting with Self: I'm All for You, Body and Soul

Remember the safety instructions on your last airplane flight? Put the oxygen mask on yourself first before assisting those travelling with you. Why? You're only useful to others after first taking care of yourself. IW means you are willing to surrender to yourself and say: "Okay, I won't interfere. This time I'll listen to YOU."

Where is the wisdom of knowledge located within? Well, actually everywhere. You think with your whole being rather than just with a specific organ. We'll begin with the brain.

The neocortex, that "new bark" (as the term means

in Latin) on the outer rim of the brain contains the area most commonly associated with cognition. The left/right division of the neocortex governs higher levels of functioning—reason, fantasy, spirituality, higher consciousness, reason, and intuition. It has two primary ways of processing things. The left generally draws conclusions based on reason and observation which are conveyed verbally. The right side processes holistically and likes to go beyond the five senses to create new contexts of reality.

The neocortex integrates with the older evolutionary parts, the mammalian and the reptilian. Each part is responsible for a different kind of function. The mammalian brain (present in lower mammals like horses and cats), governs the knowing we get through our emotions as well as aspects of bonding and relationships. The reptilian part (present in reptiles like snakes) governs automatic responses such as breathing, heartbeat, sweating, and muscle reactions. As you can see, knowing is actually a mind/body/spirit affair. The triune brain explores things with you, rather than "for" you.

Ignoring the Wisdom of Your Feelings: a Heart Bypass

You've undoubtedly left home sensing full well you've forgotten something, but couldn't "think" what it was. Your feelings gave you information which you acted upon. Or information was triggered through your senses. Perhaps you remembered (think of it: re-member, that's a body term!) through a smell, sight, sound, or taste.

The triune brain needs the integrated information from mind, body, and spirit. The problem is, we humans have learned to bypass parts of our triune brain.

Acting without awareness of the body is literally heartless, for with emotions and feelings we access knowledge as well.

The three parts of the brain have not yet learned to cooperate fully. When you tune out the body and its feeling messages, you essentially block the coordination of the triune brain.

According to Paul MacLean in the Tarrytown Letter, 1982, "The human brain suffers from a quasi-schizophrenic split between reason, emotion and survival drives, all based on inadequate integration between the neo-cortex and the older (reptilian and mammalian) brains."

The key to integration, then, seems to come from listening to feelings, emotions, and the empathic self. Your mission must thus be felt in every fiber of your being. Ingrid illustrates the consequences when the entire self—particularly the body—and her mission are not integrated:

Ingrid Ignores Body Language

A rugged and independent Swede, Ingrid had come to the U.S. from Scandinavia in the sixties with a degree in chemistry. After enjoying several good jobs with pharmaceutical companies, she landed a position with a leading aerospace corporation in southern California. Six years later, her career crashed in front of her eyes when she was laid off. In the meantime she had become a citizen and wanted to remain in the U.S. But after sending out 150 resumes and exhausting her twenty-six weeks of unemployment compensation, Ingrid despaired of ever getting off first base. Nothing seemed to work for her. (Mission was also not a working concept for her.)

I noticed that although she claimed to be depressed

211

about her lack of work ("I need a job" she would say every time I saw her), she seemed to be having a great time. She got involved in politics, did volunteer work for a couple of service organizations, read books and saw movies she'd never had time for. She had time to reflect on her life. She was in the best of moods when working on environmental projects and humanitarian issues to wile away the time.

But Ingrid rigidly refused to admit she wanted to do anything new. "Besides," she said, "I can get a good salary doing work on missiles." (Logic!) One day, Ingrid watched a movie on Mother Teresa in which Teresa exhorted people to "follow their heart." She felt an instant dizziness and pain. Without warning, she was sick all the next day. Usually a picture of health, she now couldn't get out of bed. "Was there a connection between her illness and Mother Teresa's message?" I asked. "Just coincidence," Ingrid insisted.

Her body had spoken even if she didn't listen to it. Ingrid finally got a job doing the same old thing. When she announced it, I thought she was describing a disaster that had befallen her. If her spirits were uplifted with her new position, I missed it (and she did, too).

Exercise 11.1: "ULTIMATE BEING"

This exercise helps you tap into your mind/body/spirit connection. Stand erect and still for 3–5 minutes. During this time, say everything you notice or experience in your body. If you wiggle a finger, twitch, hear something, make a gesture, sigh, or whatever, take it into your immediate awareness. As much as possible, keep in the present. You will begin to see how much your feelings and thoughts

are expressed through your body in subtle ways.
An excerpt might sound something like this:
"I'm blinking my eyes. I feel uncomfortable
doing this. I put my hand to my ear. I hear a car
go by. I am swallowing. I lower my head. I shift
back and forth from my left foot to my right foot.
I am thinking about what I am going to say. I feel
my heart beat. I am aware of tension in my lower
back. I just folded my hands. I looked down to
get an idea. I curled my little finger. I hear a car
roar by and children shouting. I am thinking about
this evening. I notice my thoughts are wandering.
I'm feeling relaxed after having read a chapter of
Naomi's book."

Do this exercise each day for several weeks.
You'll develop an awareness of how your body
reflects what you feel and think and you'll start
listening for its wisdom.

For example, body gestures provide information
about a person's thinking. Debbie, a young post-
graduate student of philosophy, avoided her feelings on just about any subject. She had thought
out her life to the max and was able to theorize
on her condition from every angle. When I attempted to get Debbie to discuss her feelings
about her mission, she invariably ran a hand
through her hair. When I asked about her habit,
she was totally unaware of it. Debbie needed to
get out of a mental straightjacket and connect to
her feelings. Her body knew she was overloaded.

Tony's Twist

Tony was a veteran of thirty years as an accountant in
a local manufacturing firm. He slumped down on the

couch, and immediately sighed about having no time for himself while turning and twisting his wedding ring. He had accepted the burden of going to work every day but was growing tired of this responsibility. Did he resent his wife staying home and not having a career? "No." (twist). Did he wish he could have some time to himself like his wife? "Yes." (twist). Could he give up his need to be the sole provider? "No." (twist). Would he consider doing something his wife would not approve of? "No." (twist). I asked Tony about his feelings of being the breadwinner. Only after I made him aware of the ring twisting did he admit that he was angry and resentful at his wife for her "easy life." How he wished he could have the luxury of six months "off." The twist became very obvious in meaning.

Had he ever wanted his wife to work before this? "No," Tony said proudly, "I felt it was my role to earn the money." Some time later, Tony admitted that the anger was really self-directed, because he had boxed not only himself in with his "sole provider" stance, but had also kept his wife from developing her mission as well.

I credit Frau Dr. Margarethe Mitscherlich of Düsseldorf, Germany, for explaining to me how she uses this technique of the "significant gesture" in her therapy. With every client she has discovered a revealing, habitual body movement which sheds light on a problem she or he was working through. We'll pursue this body language a bit further.

The Painful Truth

Body pain is an indicator of blocked energy. Like those unconscious gestures, if you listen, it can supply you with a lot of feedback. Language reflects "body wisdom": someone is a "pain in the neck," you "feel it in your gut," you don't "have the heart to do it," and so

214

forth. Rather than looking at pain as a nuisance, get in touch with that discomfort and find what it's trying to tell you. Try the following exercise.

Exercise 11.2: PROBING YOUR PAIN

Sit comfortably or lie on the floor and relax your entire body. Now scan it for any pain, discomfort, or stress. As soon as you find the greatest ache, intensify it, exaggerate it, make it as sharp as you can. While in this state, ask this part of your body for help. Become that place in your body and tell yourself what's the matter. What is the source of the pain? What does the location have to do with your life? Here are some body insights clients have come up with:

- Hearing or ear aches   — need to trust self and shut out outside influences
- Seeing problems   — need to see things clearly or blurred vision or be willing to focus on objectives
- Throat conditions   — communication problems; need to express feelings and love
- Chest pains   — need to unblock emotions; need to try softer
- Breast pain   — need for nourishment
- Back pain   — burden of having to support world; unexpressed sadness
- Colon problems   — suppressed anger

215

Pains make you think. What are your aches and pains telling you?

Carla: Flying "But"ress

Carla's PM was Analyzer with some secondary Motivator traits. She had three areas of interest: dancing, creative writing, and biology. Approaching thirty, she was terrified of not being able to make that triple combination (or any parts thereof) work. She continued her job of managing a family-owned furniture store, allotting little time to inner work. As a result, she was experiencing enormous headaches and eye trouble.

Carla felt to follow her path would be self-indulgent, (i.e., giving in to her body), although each time she wrote, danced, or took a science course she felt fine for that period of time. Besides, her family wanted her to do something "real," like go into business. Carla's devotion to "reality" was doing her in, and her body knew it.

Carla's eye trouble was the clue for her. For a long time she had been focusing her sights on the present, seeing only what her family wanted her to see. She began to direct her thoughts inward (whereupon the headaches diminished, too) and discovered she needed to attend graduate school to integrate her desires of science and writing. She began to feel a surge of energy and took up ballet once again!

Rigorous Self-Honesty Precedes Any Journey Within

Going inward demands rigorous standards of honesty and ethics. That's not so easy in a society which promotes and encourages duplicity and self-deceit. How many times have you heard "she's away from her desk"

216

and you knew it wasn't true? A favorite rejection slip from editors is: "It doesn't fit into our plans," when you know it really means "We didn't like your stuff." Irangate, Watergate—you name it—and you'll find respected officials lying blatantly and openly "in the public interest" (it's called disinformation).

A client recalled the story of his aunt and nephew sitting together in the living room watching TV. Aunt, "Is the light from the lamp bothering you?" Nephew, "No." The aunt asked the question three times but stopped when her nephew's voice quivered with irritation. She then got up, went into her bedroom, and reemerged wearing a hat with an oversized visor. The aunt deceived herself, of course. It was she, not the boy, who was irritated by the lamp.

Family communication is infrequently the paragon of forthrightness. You learn early on how to decode your parents' messages and translate them into what was actually meant. You were actually dealing with dishonesty whenever you unveiled the message. Parents may have admonished you with the question, "Who do you think you are?" But they really meant, "I don't like the way you are, and I want you to stop being that way." If you had answered "I am being myself," you might have come away with a knuckle sandwich.

How many of you have experienced honest communication with siblings and friends, either? If you have experienced much miscommunication, it will affect how you talk with yourself. You may fool some of the people some of the time, and they may fool you, but fooling yourself even some of the time will result in depression, distrust, lack of self-esteem, and a derailed mission.

217

Honesty and Life Mission

Give yourself direct, honest, and unmixed messages about what you want. Any con job you do on yourself will result in a delayed or missed mission. When I asked Rae, a successful manager of a merchandising firm, to describe how she was conning herself, she fell silent, then her face contorted as if Ramtha or John were entering her body for a channelling. Actually, Rae was making a first attempt at going within (the art of self-channelling). Staring dejectedly at the floor, she admitted that she really didn't want to be #1. "I'd rather be a good follower. I want my mission to play out behind the scenes."

It was a breakthrough for Rae. Her endless striving for the elusive laurel wreath never matched her true desires. It was her father who wanted Rae to be Ms. Prima. She freed herself from the imprisonment of the lie of competition, perfection, and being #1.

Four Clues from Your Inner Wisdom

Your inner wisdom communicates to you in uncustomary ways. How can you know when that inner wise person is at work? Look for the following clues:

1. Rewards for inner work
2. Less resistance
3. Feelings of timelessness
4. Feelings of passion

Make note of when these things occur. Keep a notebook and record the contexts. Invariably, they will happen after you have consulted with yourself. They will empower you to spend energy in the service of your mission.

218

1. Rewards for inner work. You are always rewarded for going with your inner wisdom. Be on the lookout for immediate payoffs for that internal work. It might be getting fired from a job you hate (hardly ever seen as a bonus!), it might be a phone call or an unexpected check in the mail.

Last year my partner Sue, a psychotherapist, after several years of seeing her clients grow and develop remarkably fast, decided she had to reduce her private practice by at least 50 percent. It was a difficult decision. She had spent so much on her education, had worked hard to build up her practice, and now was finally seeing a return on all that risk.

She also found it difficult to make the sad decision of whom to keep, and whom to let go. A lot of internal guidance was needed. Not ten minutes after her selections, the phone rang. One of her clients, whom she wanted to release but felt terrible about telling the decision, had already decided to relocate to another city and needed to terminate!

Now, a year later, when Sue, after inner consultations with herself, resumed a fuller practice, two old clients called up that very day to schedule appointments! Sue got instant rewards for correct decisions. There are no accidents.

2. Less resistance. When you follow your inner wisdom, things flow easier and you don't have to strain as much. When you are on your path, you will experience a smoothness you hadn't imagined possible—the Mach 1 Experience.

If you are experiencing obstacles, examine what's causing it. Is it the activity itself or another factor? For instance, I resisted this book at first, struggling and straining to get fifteen pages written. Although I knew

219

from my inner work that I must write this book, I was resisting Mach 1. I'd find excuses to do anything else but write. Everything came slowly, painfully, and reluctantly. I also learned that I needed to get a computer. I acted on that advice, although I had to borrow money for it. When I began using a computer, things literally flowed out of my hands and onto the screen.

3. Feelings of timelessness. When you go into your source and follow the advice, you will lose a sense of time. Acute awareness of time, either when it drags or races, is a sign that something is wrong. For example, when you say "time flies," you are having fun. The irony is when you are having fun you seem to have less time because it flies!

When time feels like the interval between paychecks, it can weigh you down. You look at your watch constantly and think about when you can be free. When you are bored or unhappy, time seems to drag. What a mess! Unbearable times never seem to end, but when you're having fun, time flies. (The only way to have time slow down, then, is to be bored!) That's the tyranny of thinking about time. Watch if you find yourself saying, "Time dragged on that picnic." "I wasted my time on that novel," or "I frittered away my time at the office this weekend;" examine why you engaged in these activities and try to avoid doing them.

Living according to your inner wisdom releases you from the tyranny of time. An artist friend described it this way, "When I paint, I almost step outside of time. If anything, it appears to be suspended." Only when you are acting out of desire do you have the luxury of standing outside of the tyranny of time.

Dossey cites the example of the Zen mediator who experiences five minutes of deep meditation as though it were an hour. (Maybe that's why I wouldn't meditate in the dentist's chair.) In five minutes of time, the mediator has processed a lot of information—an hour's worth. Time seems to stretch to accommodate that information, but without being a drag.

4. Feelings of passion. Your mission must give you a rush, a thrill—even an erotic feeling. Doing your soul's bidding must provide your libido with lots of stimulation and sizzle. When I ask clients what is sexy about their jobs, they usually laugh or look dumbfounded. "That's something I never really connected with work!" Why not? Who ever said jobs had to be dull, drab, tedious, and uninteresting?

Of course there will be times when things are routine, vexing valleys among the passionate peaks. A steady diet of climaxes would be too much even for the most rabid pursuer of a Life Mission. But if the erotic factor has left your career, then it means, as in a relationship, that something is missing.

Follow the Clues on Where to Spend Your Energy

Be aware of where you put your energy. Energy itself is neutral, but it can be wasted or put to good use. I found that I tended to work harder on things which were not part of my mission. If something challenged me, I piled on the effort. (Doers and Analyzers are prone to this type of behavior.) I poured time and toil into my teaching at college. I prepared endless lecture notes and read books copiously in order to be informed. The more I hated it, the harder I struggled.

Make your efforts count. If you have committed to something you do not want to do, then stop doing it!

221

It could be anything from quitting a compulsive, addictive habit, resisting the temptation to do low priority things, or terminating your job. Listen to yourself carefully.

If you like something, you'll devote time to your path and your attitude towards the process will change. You'll say: this is fun, thrilling, or, I love doing this! And the idea of spending time (an interesting concept) on it simply doesn't enter your mind. Even the less glamorous parts will be okay if the overall process is exciting. After all, renovating a house includes less fun things like cleaning up, getting rid of the trash, or ordering materials. But if it contributes to something you love, you'll not find it a drag

---

Exercise 11.3: *CREATING YOUR PERSONAL MYTH*

Myth is "a story or belief that attempts to express or explain a basic truth." Each of us has a private image of ourselves aching to be revealed. It is the truth about us as we feel it. A final stage of inner work is to redesign the person—YOU—from the inside out according to what you want her or him to be. *Create the you of your mythology.*

What is this image of your myth based upon? You can supply themes for private myth from a variety of sources. Find a character from history, lore, or literature whom you admire and who characterizes what you feel. You can also draw a picture, write a song, a poem, a description, or create an abstract collage to describe your myth.

Write down everything you can think of pertaining to the person of your mythology. Supply all the details about them. What time does she/he live in? What place, situation, or environment does this person live in? What does this person do and with whom do they associate? Do not show this to anyone. Once you get in touch within, your inner wisdom will flood you with suggestions and encouragement.

Now write a one-page description of yourself in the present tense. This is your vita sheet, in myth form. Include a statement of purpose, preferably worded in a fantastic or mythical way. Let's say your myth is that of Snow White looking for a kingdom in which to provide foster care for orphaned children. Include all the things you are capable of doing. Don't worry for now about qualifications. You don't have to know anything about magic to call yourself Merlin.

Visualize yourself being this person in your present setting, talking with your friends, working and interacting with others. Imagine how you feel when you are this person and what you can accomplish as a result. With this personal image, you could then set out to revolutionize the care of orphans. Then everyone in this world would truly whistle while they work!

Act out this myth in a ceremonial fashion. Get dressed up as this character, get cards with their name on it, act the role of the person in front of a mirror, be the person every day for an allotted period of time, call yourself by their name! Get into the part that you desire!

The more you live your myth, the easier it will be for you to become the person you want to be. This is not a con job. Your myth is the person you have been hiding from yourself! She or he is there in vibrant, pulsating color, full of energy and passion. Take off the veil of deceit and live your myth! In turn, you will become a model to yourself and to the world.

Jacques Cousteau responded to his personal myth which said to pursue three things: medicine, sailing, and film making. Instead of denying the message he devoted his life to all three: studies on the psychology and physiology of diving (medicine), travels on the ship Calypso (being a sailor), and documentaries (film making), and created the Cousteau myth we all know so well. Cousteau demonstrates that you respond to internal signals and leave the integration of desires to your wisdom. Your life can be apples and oranges—and a bowl of cherries!

When you look for guidance, be the kind of thoughtful person who never forgets to include yourself. What better source for all you need could you possibly imagine than your own self? Inquiring within is evidence of your self-love, self-trust, and self-reliance.

Poke around in the coals of a fire, stir them up and give them a puff of breath and they will rekindle. And so it is with the flame of your Life Mission. It often lies smoldering in the embers, and needs reviving. IW rekindles the passionate fire of deepest wishes, desires, and passions. Answering the call means responding to your inner fire.

We'll turn now to the gentle, soft path to assist in stoking the fire of your mission.

Chapter Twelve

Try Softer

Less is more.

—MIES VAN DER ROHE

The previous three chapters discussed the inner work of going within. This chapter emphasizes the *soft quality* of that work. *Try Softer* challenges you to use the gentle way to get results. *Try Softer* is more lasting because it operates in tune with internal wisdom, and healthier because it permits the wise use of your energy. You'll realize your mission more smoothly when you are efficient with your resources.

If you have to be in control, define outcomes, receive according to what you give, if you are into workaholism, programming results, or anything else which seeks to make things happen by sheer force of muscle or will, then this chapter is especially for you.

The Soft Truth

Much of the Western world is terminally addicted to the value of hard work. "If at first you don't succeed, try, try again" (harder, of course). Or how about Churchill's famous "Blood, sweat and tears." Or, "Work hard and you'll amount to something." "You don't get something for nothing" was the phrase I remember from home.

But just look at the enormous toll the hard approach takes on people's physical, spiritual, and emotional health. It's often referred to as Type A behavior: people chomping at the bit at traffic lights, fighting for the last car space in a parking lot, or working 60 hours a week (usually at jobs which themselves require a try-harder attitude and keeping a pace that would tire out even the most rabid workaholic). "We never took breaks," one witness in the *Iran/Contra* hearings put it. Doers are classic Type A people.

The trouble is, Type A behavior usually benefits physicians, therapists, funeral directors, cocaine dealers, and anyone else trying to patch up or put away people. One word used for drug dealers is "pusher," while booze with high alcohol content is called "hard liquor." And that's not accidental. Try Harder imposes on you and your body, *Try Softer* disposes of pain and obstacles.

The word radical means "coming from the root, to derive from the soil, to grow out of, or from something." *Try Softer* is a radical concept because it gets at the root of the Life Mission issue. If it's hard then stop doing it. Hardness means you need to change your approach.

Try Softer: *Where's the Beef?*

There are three major factors mitigating against the *Try Softer* approach: 1) cause and effect thinking; 2) hard is better (has more beef); and 3) instantmania.

Remember the county fair? There were always guys hitting a gong with a hammer. You could see the cause/ effect relationship between the force of their blows and the height of the ball—the harder they swung, the higher the ball would rise. When it came to this game, muscle seemed to work. Of course sheer strength is useful for some things like lifting heavy packages. The problem occurs when the superiority of muscle power is generalized to all endeavors.

The myth stubbornly persists that "hard" is better for everything. "Hard" means tough, beefy, macho, or durable. "Soft," on the other hand, connotes such things as wimpy, a pushover, feminine, and weak. Students hardly admit they "studied easy" for a test in school. Anyway, it would be almost anti-American! Rarely are people rewarded for doing something with grace and ease. It's as if they were going against the rules. (They are!)

The age of instant gratification and "masculine" values favors the hard way because it seems to show immediate results. The centuries-old dependency on trying harder no longer applies in realizing a Life Mission. Your Source is not impressed by the big boss approach.

Soft Is Hard (at First)

Try Softer is a principle by which you allow things to happen, events to take place, processes to unfold on their own terms. *Try Softer* relies on the *intention* and

227

direction of energy to achieve effective goals rather than fast results. Inner energy replaces cause and effect thinking and sheer force.

Try Softer uses the law of attraction. Things come to you because you have created the environment, set the stage, provided the culture so that what you need will flourish and prosper.

Caution! *Try Softer* is NOT a brand of California-style Tofu, meditation pillows accompanied by soft New Age music and mantras, with the expectation that everything is going to fall from the sky. It's a challenging business, requiring trust, surrender, and faith that the fulfillment of your desires and mission happens via the path of least resistance. Then, things appear to "just happen."

Try Softer: "*Just*" Desserts

Ever since my early teens I dreamt of going to Europe. I listened to music from foreign countries, saved my money, and began to learn German. One day, Ursula, a German exchange student in my high school, just happened to ask me to spend the following year in her home. I said yes immediately and was off to Germany that fall.

However, the stay with her family didn't work out, and I decided instead to go to Nuremburg to visit a friend of the family who had just returned to Germany from studying in the States. She had no idea I was coming to visit. Upon arrival, I discovered that she had just broken her foot and needed someone to do things around the house. Staying at her house forced me to practice German. Since she just happened to be a language teacher, she was able to help me in ways most untrained people could not. And, since she just happened to be laid up at home, I received 24-hour language instruction and became fluent in a short time.

What You Know Won't Hurt You: Be (A)ware!

You must be fully conscious that you are *Trying Softer*. During my European adventure, I didn't know I was using *Try Softer*. Every time something went my way, I found a perfectly reasonable explanation for why I got what I wanted: good old cause-and-effect stuff.

I told myself I had worked hard to save money and earn my way to Europe. Having done all the work myself, I was convinced that I deserved full credit for it. That was the Puritan ethic: you got it when you earned it. No one else contributed to my success.

So far so good. But here's the rub. Nothing ever felt easy during that time. I couldn't enjoy my stay for what it was—my Source providing! And, whenever something went wrong, I found myself obsessing over every little mistake. It felt like going upstream. Each time things worked out I breathed a huge sigh of relief. Anxiety came from a feeling that I had to control everything.

In retrospect I know I experienced *Try Softer*, even though at the time things seemed hard. It was as if I had done clothes in a washer but felt as if I had washed them by hand.

The upshot of unconscious *Try Softer* is that you can't learn from it, give it credit, nor nurture or appreciate it if you are not aware it is in operation! It needs your undivided and conscious attention.

To Do and Not to Do: That's the Answer

The *Try Softer* process is a paradoxical combination of preparation and not doing anything. A colleague of my father used to say: "God looks good when you're prepared." Well, your Source looks great if you let it operate on its own terms.

Notice that I didn't sit around waiting for things to happen to get me to Europe. In fact, there was a lot to prepare for: learning a foreign language, visualizing desires, getting a part-time job, saving money, looking into inexpensive travel, and thinking about a place to stay. The fulfillment of my vision came five years after it had entered my mind, five years of apparently "aimless" dreaming and wishing. But all of this action really wasn't hard because it was happening in the service of my mission.

The not doing part requires that you stop pushing, abandon trying to make things happen, and relinquish being in control—all non-action verbs! *"Let It Be,"* as the Beatles' song says. With *Try Softer* you are in effect saying that less achieves more. It's like hitting a golf ball in a relaxed and easy manner. It seems illogical, but that's precisely the way to do it for maximum effectiveness. Nice and easy does it every time. And the same method is true for your life.

Ways to Soften Up

Here are some softener tips you can use to undo any hardness in preparation for the *Try Softer* program I'll introduce later.

1. Examine your life. The most successful experiences of life flow easily. Individual parts may be "illogical" and setbacks can occur. That doesn't matter because the outcome will give you what you envisioned, and that's what counts. Identify one successful experience of your life, take it apart (like I did for Europe) and look at the process.

a) Trace the sequence of events. Did things "add up"? (For example, did you program things to happen in just the way they did?)
b) Did you have to work "hard" to make the events happen? When? How did you feel during those times? What did "hard" net you?
c) Was your entire experience without any setbacks? What were they?
d) When did you surrender to the process, i.e., pull instead of push?
e) During that time were you focused on the experience and the outcome you wanted from it? Was it easier than when you pushed?

2. Look for **Try Softer** *examples in others.* Ask people to tell you about their successful experiences. It makes for wonderful conversation since people love to talk about their successes. Ask why they thought things happened in the way they did. Look for the "illogical," "fantastic," or "nonsensical" aspects to their stories. Were they focused on what they wanted? Did the script go as they had expected?

A songwriter I know got his big break while selling shoes on Venice Beach. A producer chanced by and in the course of the conversation, the struggling artist mentioned that he wrote songs. "Send me a tape," said the producer. Later that week, the producer called in the middle of the night and said, "I like your songs." A record contract followed. Logical? No. If I told you the way to a song-writing mission was to sell shoes at

231

the beach, you'd say it was crazy. Precisely. Following your passion knows no logic.

Change your direction of thinking. Where you end up is where you need to be so why aim first? You are the arrow, not the archer. Let your mission take its course, and go where it needs to go.

As the poet T. Roethke said in his poem, "The Waking":

I learn by going where
I have to go.

3. Accept your Life Mission as a gift. It's easy to get presents. But do you accept the one important gift that has been given to you? You must be able to do that before you can give it to others. Only when you recognize your gift can you pass it on in the form of a career, a vocation, or pastime.

On TV the opera singer, Renata Scotto, was asked how she would like to be remembered. She said: "I would like to be remembered that on stage I always loved my audience so much and that the most important thing is the *voice was a gift that I received* that is not mine. It's something I have to share with my audience. I would like to be remembered as someone who *shared her career* with her audience." [Italics mine]

A gift is something which comes to a person. It is one which is then to be shared and given to others. *Try Softer* is receiving and accepting the gift that is yours.

Apply the five-step program below to finding your mission.

Your Five Step *Try Softer* Program:

1. Connect to Your Desire
2. Focus

3. Trust Your Source
4. Use Less is More
5. Look for Results

1. Connect to your desire. *Try Softer* depends first and foremost on letting your desire rather than muscle power carry you. You'll push less whenever you wish more. Nothing ought to be easier than saying "I want this." Closing yourself off from desires will block you from ever having them. Look at cats: they don't seem to mind asking for what they want. Learn from your furry friends and make your mission purr with your fulfilled desire.

Desire and Your PM

Each profile has differing approaches and difficulties with the desire part of the *Try Softer* process. Doers work with results, not feelings, making wishing tedious because it takes too long or is too soft. Meditation is especially helpful for you. You Motivators, on the other hand, tend to shower the world with desires and have trouble focusing on one. You think in all or nothing terms.

Stabilizers want to know each step of the way whereas desires thrive on the spontaneous and unbridled approach. Stabilizers need to be more flexible. From A to B is not always the most logical way to get to desires. Analyzers want to be right but desires cannot guarantee logic because they operate on laws different from cause and effect. Analyzers need to develop greater trust in the "irrational."

Identify anything that you strongly desire. Keep it simple and measurable. "Happiness" is too vague to

233

quantify. "One half day a week to read in the library," on the other hand, is much clearer. Other examples:

a) Three hours a week for hiking
b) A new summer business suit
c) Saturday mornings with your child

Now see yourself in the situation you desire. Example: "I'd like to visit archeological sites in Greece." How would you feel if you followed through on that wish? "Elated and invigorated!" Then write a sentence saying the reward you'll get from your desire. "I'll be able to plan my trip wisely, and know just which archeological sites to see on my next trip to Europe. And, I'll appreciate these sites much more with my knowledge."

Seizing the Moment

Operating out of your desires creates a magnet which attracts what it is you need in order to achieve specific goals. Don't work at cross-purposes with your desires (that's trying harder). "Oh, I'll just do this job that I hate for a little while longer so I can earn the money to pay the bills," or "As soon as I rack up ten years in the company, I can take early retirement and then . . ." then what? The "what" will never get addressed during a limbo period of waiting. If you don't care about your desires, then any reason is good enough to postpone them. When will the moment be right? The only moment you have is the present. Seize it!

Seeing Stars

Juanita sat impatiently on the edge of her chair when she came to see me. A dynamic and intense African-

American in her mid-thirties, she dominated the session, explaining her dissatisfaction with the progress she was making in the film industry. Although she had impressive credentials, she feared she wasn't ready for the big time. Being a woman still isn't exactly a plus in the entertainment industry. But Juanita also wasn't sure what her exact desires were, she felt she could go in a number of different directions.

She had spent a lot of time avoiding what she really desired by excessive doing. A Doer, Juanita didn't like to sit still very long. She had to shoot for the top emotionally before she could make anything happen. But that wasn't doing anything, she insisted. Since nothing else had worked, what could she lose? She spent the next month concentrating on clarifying desires.

They included a higher-level management position and work on a foreign film project in India. Soon she got an interview for a high-level job in a well-known entertainment firm. Her interviewers only had to see her for the rest to be history. Recently Juanita called me to say she got the job. "It's everything we talked about," she told me on the phone. "I'm really excited. As you said, 'Seeds I plant sprout daily.'"

Desires manifest when you stick with them. When clients finally connect to what they want, they say: "You'll never guess what happened to me!" "Just by chance I was doing such and such," "A funny thing happened to me," or "Out of nowhere this person called (showed, popped) up." I listen with an inner smile because it's evidence that their desires have brought results.

2. Focus. Focusing requires the commitment and concentration of all your energy on what you desire. It also helps translate your vision into something vividly recognizable, passionately dear, and intensely close. I remember going to a friend's house to see her slides of Europe. Most of them were blurred. Was that the Eiffel Tower or the watchtower at the East German border? The few pictures in focus were a relief because we could recognize what we were seeing! Then we could devote attention to the slide.

Exercise 12.1: THE EYES HAVE IT

1. Take a common object and spend two minutes inspecting every detail; look at how the light strikes it, how it feels, smells, tastes, and sounds. Look at the shape, size, texture, color, and volume of the object. Then, put your choice away and recreate it in your mind with as much detail as possible. At first, you may overlook obvious details. In time you'll discover you are more attentive to seemingly unimportant features of an object.

2. Practice the exercise twice at least three times a week.

3. Focusing attention on something will increase your interest in it. After practicing a week, pick one of your objects and write a page expressing the feelings you have for this object. Laura went on and on about paper for three pages! She knew more about types, uses, origins, manufacture, and selection than anyone would even care to know. As it turned out, paper was an emotional issue for her, and she had never suspected it until she focused. "Who would have thought," Laura said, "that I was harboring such passions!" And she had resisted the exercise up to one hour before we met. Don't thumb your nose at a common object. There is a woman who is so passionate about rubber bands that she now commands a six-figure income by importing them to the U.S.

The application of these exercises to your Life Mission development fine tunes your focus and increases your desire for this mission. When you are looking at a diamond you'd like to purchase, you focus your attention on each facet. Treat your Life Mission the same way. It's precious, just like the diamond. Focus your attention and love on it!

It would be frustrating to hear someone tell you, "I love you but I don't know exactly why." *Be clear about what you desire and focus on it.* Then and only then can you realize what you want.

Focus and Your PM

Focusing for Motivators is particularly difficult. They have so many projects and dreams to fulfill. To give up any one of them is like losing an arm. Doers are often impatient with concentrating on goals (or objects). Analyzers can focus much easier (almost to a fault) and Stabilizers must assert their need for concentrating on their desires.

"Yes, but . . ."

Cindy, a free-lance cartoonist, looked at me uncomfortably through her horn-rimmed glasses when I asked her to focus on what she wanted. A serious, articulate, and precise woman in her mid-thirties, she seemed to be the kind of woman who had the skill to achieve

237

whatever she wanted. But, every time I asked her to describe a desire, she began only to stop in midstream with, "But I know I won't get that" or "But I'll have to settle for a small beach shack instead of a studio overlooking the ocean." We went through about twenty minutes interrupted by "buts."

Cindy's parents had contributed to the pattern by saying she could do anything she wanted in life—which meant that they were giving unfocused advice. All her life Cindy had looked for things to do which were difficult so she could prove she could "do anything." In the meantime, her desire had been kept at bay. Then she would skip to something else only to repeat the process.

I suggested that Cindy review how often she blurred her desires during the week. First she was to focus on the one thing she most wanted. Then she was to complete that wish before going on to another one. First wish: enrolling in a design course at a local college. Cindy had never allowed herself to focus on that. She called up the next day for registration information.

3. Trust your Source. A key player in the *Try Softer* method is your Source. Think of your Source as a loving attendant or clerk, in the business of serving the "customer": YOU. It is there to receive directions and carry out your wishes in a non-judgmental way. If you ordered from a catalogue and said to a clerk, "I'd like something, but I don't know what," you'd get a puzzled look. The clerk needs specific information as to item, page, size, color, price, style, and whatever else is relevant.

Your Source needs conscious visions, not vagaries or pot-shot wishes. It recognizes what you need but is not in the position to be the decision maker without your consent.

To tell a person what they need before they are ready

is to ensure either confusion, resistance, or a disruption of the process. Would you like a clerk to tell you what you want before you even know what it is? You must give the green light before that clerk can proceed. The same is true of your Source which, paradoxically, operates in your best interest only if given specific desires and permission to carry them out. That's where trust comes in.

It's not easy to turn over management to someone else (especially for Doers). But *Try Softer* involves surrendering your questions and concerns to your Source. It is there at your beck and call, ready when you are. Ask for guidance and encouragement—that's doing it the easy way. When you give up the need to control the outcome or to dominate the process, then your Source has room to figure out the best plan.

4. Use Less is More. Pick an appropriately safe area to practice this step. Less is More in paying bills might not endear you to your creditors. Try something in an area where you may have been successful, but pushed a lot. Make sure you like whatever the activity is, but choose one where you haven't gotten the results you want. You may feel like you're in neutral when you'd like to go into fourth gear. But remember, idling, not driving hard, is what we're talking about here.

Remaining Speechless

Brad decided to apply *Try Softer* to speech-making. An amiable, ambitious, worried looking man in his mid-fifties, he described his shift from university teaching to public speaking. But, he complained anxiously, no matter how often he gave speeches, their quality hadn't improved much. He enjoyed talking and was good at it, but got bogged down in preparation. He remembered that at the university he had also spent a great deal of time on his lectures. A pattern!

I asked Brad to review his most successful presentations. His worried face began to lighten as he reflected that most of them had been spontaneous, with very little practice. To his surprise, the feedback he got was always quite good. "I substituted for some instructors from time to time and did quite well, considering the fact that I had no advance notice," he grinned. "And then there were the times," he continued, "that I 'winged it' for my own classes. Instead of being a dreadful flop, the session actually went over better than usual!" I asked Brad to apply the same process to giving speeches.

Brad waited until his next speaking engagement to experiment with some *Try Softer* methods of speechmaking. Every time he wanted to jot down some notes or say something into the tape recorder, he reminded himself to refrain from fully preparing the speech. He simplified his outline, identifying three main points to get across and visualized the speech and a (thunderous) audience reaction. He avoided all further preparation.

The next time I saw him, Brad was beaming. The anxious, withdrawn expression on his face had disappeared. "The reception to my last speech bowled me over," he announced proudly. Brad now worked on the speech spontaneously.

The interaction between Brad and the audience was alive, direct, and electric. No one knew of his experiment, of course. Brad figured it out: "People saw my willingness to risk and go with the moment. It was a relief not to have that obsessing beforehand."

Brad's *Try Softer* method was a new way of being rather than doing. His success impressed upon him the need to include spontaneous motivation in his mission. He received three further speaking engagements from this one speech alone.

240

5. *Look for results.* If you have been specific in
your desire, focused, and let go of the process, you
will find the yield much more than you could ever
imagine. Like Brad, you will see an increase in the
success of your project and a decrease in the effort you
put into it, and it's more fun in the process!
Practice less is more now! Maybe it's time, for instance, to put this book down and take a break. Go
out and smell the fresh air or listen to the birds sing.
Treat yourself to an ice cream cone (Tofutti if you live
in California). Lubricate your soul by loosening the
brittle, exhausting way you have been approaching
things. Then you will see desires flow, the struggle
release its grip on you, and, like the clay on the potter's
wheel, your mission will take new shape.
It all comes out in the wash: when you begin to use
softeners, things get smoother. Check it out for yourself. When did you push and when did you allow things
to work for you? Which was more successful? Give
yourself enough of *Try Softer* and you'll wonder why
you ever tried any other way. The most difficult lesson
is to go soft on yourself!
Stop the macho-muscle-manic approach. Instead of
wasting your precious energy on agenda not meant for
you, honor the softness of your path *now*!
To return to the poem by T. Roethke:

Of those so close beside me, which are you?
God bless the Ground! I shall walk softly there,
And learn by going where I have to go.

That's *Try Softer* in action!

Chapter Thirteen

Yield to Your Intuition

*"Intuit? I'm not into it," said the
left brain to the right.*

C ompare items A with B, and pick the one you
prefer.

A		B
1. ___ what I see		___ what I feel
2. ___ the present		___ the future
3. ___ solving problems by experience		___ solving problems by ingenuity
4. ___ using things		___ designing things
5. ___ what I know		___ what I find
6. ___ working with facts		___ working with hunches
7. ___ controlling the situation		___ going with the flow
8. ___ the steps of a process		___ the purpose of a process

9. ___ things as they are   ___ things as they could be
10. ___ right and wrong   ___ ambiguous situations
         situations

Total ___   Total ___

If you chose more answers on the left, (A), you're probably someone who feels intuition is about as easy to come by as a taco in Russia. If most of your check marks were on the right, (B), you're the person who can *figure out* where that Russian taco can be obtained.

Preferring the intuitive approach (right column) doesn't make you superior over the person who prefers the rational way. There is, however, an advantage for the intuitive person: free access to internal information unavailable from any other source. What could be more exciting than to access the incredible wisdom stored within you? And like a radio program, this intuition is available the moment you turn it on and tune it in.

This chapter shows how to access your marvelous resource of intuition and put it in the service of your mission. Also, it identifies the barriers to intuition and how to overcome them. And finally, it examines the relationships between intuition, Life Mission, self-acceptance, trust, and surrender.

Intuition Defined

Intuition, according to Webster, is a "direct perception of truth, or fact, independent of any reasoning process, a keen and quick insight." It is a quality that goes beyond the five senses and immediate perceptions, a conduit from your interior which conveys a direct, singular, intense, and unmistakable message when it connects to your consciousness. It has been variously described as a "hunch," a "gut feeling," a "funny sen-

243

sation deep inside," a "knowledge that goes beyond all understanding," or "illumination." No matter what you call intuition, it is an invaluable consultant to you in your Life Mission search.

Many people think that intuition is for women, creative types, artists, or gypsies. Everybody is intuitive, yet many fail to take full advantage of it. You don't need special faculties to use your own source of knowledge, just tools to discover it.

Intuition and Mission: Insider Trading

Too much "outsight" detracts from your mission. Intuition keeps you internally grounded and in tune with your subconscious self. Insight, as the word connotes, is internal vision. Since a mission can come only from within you, it is axiomatic that intuition—since it comes from the same inner source—is the font of answers to your quest. It is a private exchange of communication between you and yourself. This is insider trading that's good!

With your intuition, you will access your precise internal areas of interest, desire, and expertise. You will discover that intuition likes nothing better than to give inside guidance, advice, secrets, information, and help on matters of importance to you, such as your mission. Listening to your intuition will automatically connect you with that calling. In fact, the areas in which you get greatest intuitive insights will always pertain to your mission.

Intuition: Body Language

Common to all these descriptions is the fact that intuition operates through feelings and desires on a psy-

244

cho-physical level. The knowledge it imparts occurs through sensations, desires, emotions, and feelings. As I discussed in the previous chapter, in order to yield to intuition, you must be comfortable with your body as the source of this special kind of wisdom. Mission and intuition will seem like ships passing each other in the night if their inner connectedness does not reach your conscious self. It is imperative, then, to risk yielding to the one resource which can enlighten and reveal your desires on a conscious level.

Using intuition is like going out on a limb. But that's where the fruit is! The real risk is ignoring intuition. Use it and you'll find the limb—and exactly the piece of fruit you want.

Intuition: Who Is into It

Intuition is a lot like sex in that it's a major factor in life, but at the same time people are reluctant to talk about it. Why keep it hush-hush? Intuition has been verified by people in all walks of life from every century. It is a quality unique to humankind and one of your most important endowments.

Lawrence Loewy, the daughter of designer Raymond Loewy, related to an interviewer that after her father had finished his conceptualization of the Studebaker automobile, he turned off the lights, put some jazz on the phonograph, and ran his hands along the clay model. He wanted feel and intuition to have the final word in the car's design. Einstein regularly used his intuition before cross-checking results with his logical side. General Patton, too, patently consulted his intuition before making critical campaign decisions in World War II. And a CEO of a midwest corporation started a day-care center at his company because he

245

"figured" it would help increase worker productivity. (Self-evident, you say? How many companies do you know that have day care?)

But we don't need famous people to validate intuition. In every workshop I have ever done on creativity, participants tell fascinating stories of how they have used their intuition in business, at home, on trips, in relationships, and in virtually every situation of human life.

The Dual Role of Intuition

Intuition is powerful because it serves a dual function. It provides a storehouse of individual wisdom AND a pipeline to universal knowledge. Who doesn't like a bargain? In accessing intuition you receive a double return on your investment: *collective knowledge made particular* to your situation. The following anecdote will show how remarkably this two-for-one deal works:

"Unser Steinwald"

Several years ago, I went on a trip with Sue, my partner, and her mother Eunice. Eunice's desire was to locate the place where her brother Dane had been killed in World War II. Although he was buried in Epinal west of Alsace, Eunice thought Dane had died somewhere to the east, near Colmar. She had only the name of the forest, Steinwald, where the battle that took his life occurred. (The Alsace is an area in France where German had been the dominant language until 1918.)

When we visited Dane's grave at the U.S. cemetery, I checked the battle records, but I was only able to come up with some names of Alsatian towns through which Dane might have passed during the campaign.

246

Eunice talked about an area around Colmar, but that didn't feel right to me. Somehow, I thought it had to be further north around Strasbourg, close to the Rhine. We had just driven through that section on the way south, and I remember feeling a prickly sensation in my stomach when I saw a sign for the Alsatian town of Gambsheim, but I gave it no further heed. We couldn't find the Steinwald forest around Colmar, and all inquiries were to no avail.

We headed back north in the direction of Strasbourg, comforted by the fact that Eunice had at least seen Dane's military grave. I still felt that Steinwald forest was located in an area north of Strasbourg, but since time was running out before we had to return to the airport in Frankfurt, the chances of verifying this hunch seemed bleak. But my sensation that we were near Steinwald persisted even though there was no evidence of such a forest even on detailed maps of the Strasbourg area. I was going on pure intuition.

There was only time to visit one of the three Alsatian villages. I had no proof that any of them was correct, but I felt guided that one was it. After deliberating over the names of each village, I picked the one which sounded right to me—Gambsheim. Then I gave Eunice the names, and asked her to choose. "Gambsheim," she said without hesitation. I knew that funny-sounding town was it. At that moment I recalled the sensation I felt when I saw the sign a few days earlier.

As we neared Gambsheim, I glanced over my shoulder at a small patch of trees and felt goose bumps on my arms. We passed into the village, only to discover it was noontime and the streets were deserted. (In France the midday rest period lasts until 3 P.M.) I was not about to go up to a house and disturb anyone's lunch. Perhaps somebody would be on the street—an

247

old person who had survived the war and was a native speaker of German. Suddenly, we rounded a corner and saw a prim looking old man dressed in black, resting on his cane. "Stop the car!" I shouted. Had the old gentleman heard of a forest called Steinwald? *"Unser Steinwald!"* he exclaimed in German ("our Steinwald forest"). I was overjoyed, and Eunice, who understood no German, gasped from the back seat as she heard the magic word.

After getting directions, we drove straight over to the forest, pulled off the road and looked in silence at the kaleidoscope of trees, now so quiet and resplendent with fall colors. For the next half hour Eunice walked through the forest, taking in the place where her brother had spent his last few hours. It was a moment of sadness and yet extreme satisfaction. Her search had been successful. Later, I checked the local Michelin map for the area, and located a tiny green patch, not more than an eighth of an inch, just outside of Gambsheim. Too tiny for a name. But it was *"unser Steinwald."*

Gambsheim would be etched in my memory forever as the validation of intuition. Eunice and I had listened to it, and what a yield it had given! Where did our shared knowledge come from? From universal wisdom, the same collective repository where all available information is registered.

Blocks to Your Intuition

The pressure in our society to conform to logic and facts is enormous. For that reason intuition often stays under cover. No wonder, then, that you might be reluctant to use it. I have identified some common blocks which contribute to an underuse of intuition:

- Distrust
- Difficulty with Self-Acceptance
- Fear of Intuition
- Need for Control
- Giving in to the Pressure of Others

Distrust

There is a certain uneasiness about intuition, even for those using it. Imagine a coach saying, "Smith, you go in for Jones. I intuit that you can win the game for us." But in their books and private memoirs, almost all sports figures admit to relying on intuition heavily. The word itself is problematic. "Hunch" or "gut feeling" are more macho and acceptable words for the same thing. Imagine General Patton, who studied Napoleon and the Greeks extensively, using the word intuition when urging his boys on to battle (although as I mentioned, that is exactly how he made many of his major decisions).

Many people distrust their intuitive wisdom, too, because it seems too easy or elusive. Anything which comes effortlessly is greeted with suspicion. (See Chapter 12!) I remember my old Latin teacher's phrase on the board: *Ad astra per aspera!* (To the stars through difficulty.) Nothing comes easy!

Clients have dismissed their intuitive insights because they came without struggle! They weren't comfortable with short cuts that come to them like manna from heaven (except if they happened to be Moses in Egypt). Moreover, they argue, if they do trust intuition, will it provide tangible results? Too many people opt for the "sure thing" of logic rather than the greater yield from intuition. A bird in the hand seems better than two in the bush.

249

Difficulty with Self-Acceptance

How can your internal self go wrong? Only when you lack trust in its wisdom. Intuition is a part of you. All those messages you got about inadequacy reinforce a distrust of any internal messages. The tape runs something like this, "Why would I want to consult with myself? I'm not worth the trouble. I don't have the knowledge, I can't possibly know the facts," and so on. Better stick with the safe stuff, like $2 + 2 = 4$. Take the two parts: distrust of self and the distrust of the intuitive process, put them together and you've cooked up a marvelous *pièce de résistance.*

Fear of Intuition

You may tend to use your intuition to a certain point, but when you begin to see things in powerful ways you stop. I am reminded of a Schiller poem about the veil of Isis behind which truth lies hidden. A servant rushes in, lifts the veil, sees truth, and dies. (A similar theme in romantic poetry involves death for the person who sees pure beauty.)

The same sort of fear exists with intuition. I've observed that clients become uneasy when they begin to consult their intuition intimately. When they listen to their intuitive voice on Life Mission matters, they get information which they have often denied or ignored.

By not listening to intuition you can fool yourself into thinking you lack information. It becomes a vicious circle, because the fear of hearing the truth mounts with avoidance.

Many, too, are paralyzed by the thought of acting on their internal wisdom. When you know you are empowered, but then you have to act on it.

You can't lose by following your intuition! Because it is an integral part of you, it cannot be used against you. Only your interpretation of intuition can be misleading. Intuition is not the culprit, but rather fear of facing the truth about yourself. Why?

Well, you will learn about the good and the bad (intuition doesn't make judgments): your self-deceptions, compromises, relationships, jobs, mates, and talents in a more holistic, congruent way. Any contradictions, discrepancies, and dishonesty within you will now become glaringly apparent.

If my intuition tells me to sever a relationship, but that the break-up would conflict with my job, then I'll need to come clean with myself as to why I am staying in that job! Is it part of my mission path or just a security blanket connected to a relationship?

The resulting illumination (literally making light what was dark for you) will demand a response, and that's the scary part.

Need for Control

Sticking to one way of doing things or one-answer solutions can be a difficult habit to break. The need to be in control is one of the most powerful addictions in society. If you are a person who sees things in terms of right and wrong, one way and one way only (Stabilizers often do), you will be wary of your intuition and tend to shy away from its seemingly ambiguous nature. When you use logic, you avoid choice, as logic must perform in a single-minded way. But logic doesn't give information about what you want or what you desire because it doesn't deal with feelings. If you have spent $30,000 getting a degree in accounting, and you never liked the subject, what's logical about continuing to pursue it?

251

As my father used to say, "I may not always be right, but I'm never wrong." When you yield to your intuition, in effect you relinquish control (and dependency on logic) by surrendering to forces inside yourself. You dance on the crest of your own power to achieve your desires.

Laura's Hot Flash

A young, bright and energetic woman, Laura had taken an office manager position, although she had a degree in journalism. She felt that was the "logical way" to make money. Laura didn't believe that intuition gives insight on what a person should be doing. I asked her to compare two successful things she had done. She picked 1) finding a job and 2) getting an article published. To get the job, Laura went from agency to agency, newspaper ad to newspaper ad, exhaustively looking for anything which would pay her enough. "Well," she declared, "I reasoned that if I researched it long enough, I'd get what I wanted." She eventually got a position after three months.

Her article, on the other hand, was published quickly. While she was meditating, she flashed on the magazine where she would submit her article, and she got information on the format and slant it was to have. She called the editor of that magazine and was hired to write the article on the spot. She did not have to call dozens of editors. Instead she allowed her intuition to tell her which one to contact.

Her goals were the same with each project; she knew what she wanted and knew she was going to get it. The difference between the job and the magazine lay in her method of getting the results that she achieved. Getting the article published was easy because her intuition had offered advice (and she was open to it). The response to her writing gave Laura pause. Shortly thereafter, she began an in-house newsletter for her company.

The job and the article took about the same length of time to complete successfully. The car search seemed to take control of Laura. Her logic demanded a rigid sequence. If she called x number of agencies in x amount of time, she would find her job eventually, she reasoned. Her intuitive project, on the other hand, had no strict guideposts along the way and she finished the article with ease. No muss, no fuss, no bother. Laura had done the groundwork, listened to her "illogical" self and followed the information from within. She hadn't pushed; instead, she had given intuition space and opportunity to provide the way and the tools.

But even if intuition took just as long as logic, would you rather push for twenty minutes or attract things for the same amount of time?

Giving In to Group Pressure

Friendly intuition can falter under the test of group pressure. In an experiment, five people were seated in a darkened room and shown slides of four colored columns of various lengths. Their objective was to determine which column was longest. At first the four columns were obviously very different in length, and all subjects agreed as to the correct answer. But as the experiment progressed, they became increasingly similar in length.

Four of the five participants had been told what answers to give. When the four stooges gave the first obviously wrong answer, the unsuspecting participant hesitated but stuck to his own answer. Thereafter, the stooges always agreed unanimously about the "correct" answer. Soon the unsuspecting person changed his mind to agree with the others' answers. He didn't trust his own judgment. How much opportunity would your intuition have in situations when it is pitted against reason? Intuition is a solitary endeavor; you need to ignore the cries of the crowd and listen only to your voice within.

Five Ways to Tap Your Intuition

1. Practice daily. Intuition needs exercise, just like anything else. You can do mini practice sessions as well as structured, longer ones. The next time the phone rings, try to guess who it might be, or anticipate what the nature of that phone call will be. Hocus-pocus? No, that's what intuition is, simply knowing a little more fully about things beyond the facts. Keep notes on what interests you. Let's say it's buying a car. Then when you get around to your purchase, your intuition will be better informed to help you make a decision because you have done your preparation. Your intuition always looks better if you have done your homework.

Guess what people are going to say before they do. Sometimes you'll even be able to predict individual words. Have someone open a magazine to a picture and without looking, try to describe what is on the picture. Keep a log of your answers. Think of someone you'd like to hear from, and wait to see if they contact you. Ask that person how they happened to think of you.

You can also identify an object hidden in a box. Use any feelings, words, or associations which come up for you as clues. "Chubby toes," Edith, a workshop participant, blurted out while gazing at the box. She felt the object must be something owned by a person with chubby toes. A small piece of jewelry came to mind. She knew only one person with chubby toes. And that person wore a very distinctive ring. Edith guessed "ring." The object in the box was indeed a ring.

Follow up on your hunches, particularly when they are "illogical" yet persistent.

Sandy's Sixth Sense

Sandy, a single mother with two kids, woke one morning with an inexplicable urge to go halfway across town on a weekday to have a cappuccino before work. "But you usually jog in the morning," she protested to herself. Yet the urge wouldn't leave her. She knew there was a reason, even if she couldn't figure it out at the moment. So she scrapped the jogging and went in her 1976 Mazda to a little coffee house in the Marina. While sitting over the cappuccino and writing a letter to her mother, she tried to figure out why she had come. She knew it wasn't really to have coffee or communicate with her mom. But why was she there?

Just then a Dodge van pulled into the parking lot. "Gee, just like the one I'd thought about getting for me and the kids," she sighed. As the driver turned the van into a parking space, Sandy could make out the For Sale sign pasted on the window. She dashed out and looked it over. It was outfitted for camping, complete with toilet, sink, fridge, TV, and three beds, just what she had always wanted. She asked the owner what his asking price was. "Actually," the man shrugged, "I hadn't thought of a sale. I'm really looking for a small car in trade. A Mazda or something from around the same year."

"It's a deal—I've got a 1976 Mazda!" Sandy exclaimed. Within an hour they had made the trade. "So

255

it wasn't really the cappuccino!" she said to me. "It was my intuition that told me to go there. I know now when it speaks, I don't ask why. I just follow it!"

2. *Observe a lot.* Intuition comes through an ability to interpret information inside and outside you. Indeed, the only way to intuit is to tune in. You'll need to devote keen attention to what you are feeling and desiring. Ask other people how they use their intuition and when it has worked for them. Imagine using this as a party opener: "Hi! How's your intuition been doing?"

Watch how you come to know about things, and keep a journal about it. Give yourself credit when you observe correctly. When things don't turn out the way you thought you intuited them, identify the source of the confusion. Read about how people have used their intuition.

3. *Trust your intuition to be the source of truth.*
Your own day-to-day information comes from individual perceptions, awarenesses, visual and aural fields; in short, to whatever you give your immediate attention. Two people can have differing views of an event because each is coming from their own limited perspective. Intuition transcends personal limitations and perceptions to access a universal source of truth (witness *"unser Steinwald"*).

We all know someone who took a job even if they felt in their gut it was wrong. Did that job ever turn out right? Doubtful. But what made you pick up this book? You had a feeling it would do you some good. (My intuition tells me you're right.)

If there is a discrepancy between what your intuition

tells you and what you think is logical, practice going with your feelings even if the facts to back them up are not evident (remember Sandy's example). Work with low-risk items at first. Don't start by using your intuition to put all your fortune in a certain stock or quit your job.

4. Make connections. Observe the times when you link two things together "accidentally" or coincidentally. For example, how often do you think of someone and that person turns up in your life? A friend recorded at least ten "accidental" occurrences in four days, including a phone call from someone he was just thinking about, but whom he hadn't talked to in over two years. How about that new word you just learned which crops up again later in the day?

Intuition connects you to a knowledge that is pure, unhampered by restrictions, and shared by more than one person at any given time. That is why Eunice and I both could come up with Gambsheim! We were connecting to our mutual source.

5. Listen to your intuition. Go deep inside to a place where only you can talk with you. When you lend an ear, you will find intuition to be your soul-mate, your guide, and your counselor. What do you really need to be in your life? How do you make use of your gift? Intuition will gently guide you. If you drop the "shoulds" and "ought-tos," intuition may even be able to help you forget the "reasonable" way to be. I must emphasize again that most people are not overwhelmed by what their intuition says, but by the prospect of following through on it!

Listen to yourself as you would listen to a loved one. Let that voice implore, beseech, motivate, cajole, and otherwise cause you to rise up, throw off any burden of guilt and fear, and follow your own voice. Be your own Pied Piper and dance to your own intuitive melody! Intuition is that vital, generous, and necessary partner to which we all have the luxury of access.

Pursue your necessary luxury.

Part Three

MISSION ACCOMPLISHED

Chapter Fourteen

Mission Accomplished

It's the gift to be simple
It's the gift to be free
It's the gift to come down where you ought to be
And when you find the place just right
You'll be in the land of love and delight.

—SHAKER HYMN

This book begins and ends with gifts. They're really quite simple. You don't need to write a doctoral thesis or paint the Sistine Chapel to prove you have them. Take Martha, who wanted to beautify the environment, Gene, who wanted to farm, and Danny, who found his mission nurturing young people. Ordinary stuff, so much so that you almost wonder what all the fuss is about. The extraordinary thing about them is that they followed through on their calling. They "came down where they ought to be."

You'll reach that "land of love and delight" the Shakers sang about if you keep these simple ideas in mind:

1) Everyone has a gift.
2) You, too, have a gift, and it is special.

Finding Your Life Mission

3) Your gift is within.
4) You are responsible for finding out what it is.
5) Accept your gift fully.
6) Give your particular gift back to the world.
7) Use your gift and you'll "come down where you ought to be."

The core of your mission is that simple gift you receive and pass on. It is your beacon, anchor, and path. It's what you are here for.

If you haven't yet "found the place just right," take heart. If you go on the quest of discovery you'll reach your mission as surely as the people in this book did. Your calling is an ongoing process. How you express it may differ from stage to stage in your life. There will always be new dimensions, new insights, and fresh starts. But the theme of your life will be your constant companion and support through any and all change.

Being willing to go through any difficulty *individually* is the first step. No one can meet and fulfill your Life Mission challenge except you. Friends may offer advice and mates encouragement, but the final decision will be yours. If you make it for reasons other than yourself, you are saying that others' agendas are more important than your own. There is a difference between taking something into account and doing something on account of someone else. You must know and understand that difference.

If you think you have neglected your Life Mission up to now, take heart. When you picked up this book, you might have been experiencing a time of contraction, a sense of being "off track." The paradox is that you are never off track! It takes time before you can expand your lungs when they are contracted. That's a simple law of nature. So contraction always precedes

262

expansion. Your mission gives you the power to inspire yourself and others. It allows you to breathe in (*inspire* in fact means to breathe in) and experience expansion. Let's look at one final example. Elizabeth R. is a woman who met the challenge and realized her mission. Observe how she managed her exercises and tasks, how she dealt with fears and discomfort, how she kept on going in spite of resistance from others, and how she overcame negative thoughts. Notice her PM and how she approached her goals as a result.

Elizabeth: From Resister to Sister

A wiry 54-year-old woman with graying hair, Elizabeth was a Division Head of a computer research firm. She characterized her dilemma this way: "I was having lunch with one of the CEO's in the executive dining room overlooking the entire city. I had everything I wanted, but I felt an emptiness inside."

Elizabeth had taken at least a half-dozen career tests (she was a Stabilizer with some secondary Analyzer traits) but felt none the wiser. Burned out and unhappy in the city where she was living, she was despondent because she feared, and thus resisted, change. She thought a new job would never bring her the salary she was presently commanding. If she relocated, she thought it would disrupt her partner's work.

Elizabeth explored her interests, her past, her needs, and worked intensely on her desires. She kept a copious journal, wrote about her past, and taped her thoughts. She realized that her mission had always dealt with doing quiet things which bring people closer together. Words and phrases like "big band playing on the lake," "summers on the farm," and "family photos" came up in her journals. She still felt the attraction to technology, but now more in the service of communications.

263

Her fondest hope was to move closer to her sister in Illinois. Elizabeth's need for a haven, for closeness to the community where she had grown up, and for a closer bond with her sister was almost stronger than her career. But as she realized, those desires were related to her choice of work and characteristic of her PM! Once she accepted those needs as "okay" she could affirm them and make them come true.

For a Stabilizer type, any change creates anxiety, and has to be prepared for carefully. Self-employment for Elizabeth turned out to be an unlikely option because she needed security. If that wasn't enough, she and her partner were unable to sell their house because of the slow real estate market at the time.

Then Elizabeth made some further attitudinal changes. She decided first to give up the attachment to the house that was chaining her to her present city of employment and job. Then she identified the changes she wanted to make. She wanted to work for a firm which manufactured products to foster communication in an atmosphere less demanding and stressful than her present position.

Elizabeth was able to feel, taste, experience, and smell the location she wanted. All of a sudden, a number of astonishing things happened: 1) She received a job offer from an optics firm in a town near her mother; 2) Although housing was tight, the house right next to her sister was put on the market to lease! 3) It was possible for her to take the job offer without undue financial strain; 4) Suddenly Elizabeth's house sold; and 5) Her partner was able to continue a career in the new location.

All of the above happened within a month. The optics firm rekindled Elizabeth's love of photography. Soon she began a small portrait business, and in just three years expanded it to a full-time business with her partner.

Within three months she went from the despair of ever getting what she wanted to having a splendid outcome to her wishes. She never stopped pursuing her dreams in spite of recurring doubts and fears. She trusted her inner wisdom and the guidance of her Source. It was a joy to see Elizabeth's face as she got the news of her transfer. Although I was sorry to bid her farewell, I knew it was right for her.

Sorry, Wrong Number . . .

Wherever you turn, there are examples of missions never undertaken, never fulfilled, never realized, or gone haywire. Hitler's attempts to gain (self-)acceptance as an artist is an infamous example that comes to mind.

But you don't need well-known people to find examples. People with missed callings languish all around: the neighbor who never got beyond all those years of child-bearing, your brother who could have reached for the stars but stayed on safe ground to carry on the family tradition, that brilliant, eccentric aunt who stayed in a menial job and provided gossip at family reunions, or a high school friend whose talents were obvious to everybody but him.

Contrast these sad examples with those people who have been shining lights. Perhaps there was a teacher who inspired you to bring out a hidden talent, a person in your community who never seemed to stop making waves, or perhaps a relative who quietly followed his dreams and became an example for you.

A Look into the Future

What would the world be like if right from the start people were totally involved with pursuing a dream uniquely theirs? How would the world look if everyone lived a mission with determined passion and unencumbered joy? What would the emotional, economic, and societal effect on all of us be, if people were not running away from something but rather towards the realization of their desires?

More to the point, how would that world look if it were *harvesting the fruits of your calling?* Try for a moment to imagine your gift spreading out into the world, seeing your gift working for global good. Here's my vision of how the planet will look when your gift (indeed everyone's gift) becomes global.

The planet will hum. You'll devote time, money, energy, and resources to the things you need to fulfill your dreams. You'll know your priorities because you've identified your own needs.

You'll trust your decisions and take greater risks to meet them as you begin to use your Source for guidance. You'll no longer be going through the motions of driving listlessly to work in the service of earning money. Instead, you'll "come down where you want to be" to complete a specific assignment in the service of your mission.

When you feel the effects of responding to your inner calling, you'll want to pass the torch and encourage others to find their own mission.

When you are living your own mission, there will be no need to aggress against others out of feelings of deprivation. No need to see the world in terms of "you have what I want." *Lebensraum,* new frontiers, expansion, exploration, and discovery of new worlds will

266

refer to a *conquest of space within yourself* rather than of property, people, or land. You'll feel the need to give of the overflowing gift that you have rather than envy what someone else has.

You will learn how to *attract* the good to yourself, rather than push to make it come to you. When you manifest your mission, your life will be more harmonious, congruent, and conflict-free. Values such as pursuing the latest fad, keeping up with the Yuppies (or whatever is the current buzz word), wearing a certain style because that's what one does, will no longer matter.

Since you are responsible for your space and are working on your own agenda, you'll not be concerned with what others are doing. Any need to do things on the behalf of others will not come at the beginning of the decision-making process, but as a result of making decisions for your own benefit. In meeting your own needs, you'll be the ultimate beneficiary of your choice.

Paradoxically, you'll now be able to respond to the needs of others more compassionately because you can detach yourself from feelings of competition and envy. And you will model the thrill of a fulfilled mission and its benefits to others. They, in turn, will feel no need to protest that you are being selfish and ignoring them because they'll have met their own needs. These people will recognize that you need to be going in a different direction. Mates will listen to your dreams and support your passions, and offspring or siblings will encourage you to stop living through others and become yourself.

When you live your mission, you'll have options and choices rather than restrictions and closed doors. You will make clear and positive decisions based on your desires. Your creativity and fantasy will thrive, as you have more time to explore and invent things. You'll

267

spend more time on developing your intuition because you'll see it as a necessary partner in the mission process.

You'll eagerly spend time with yourself and you'll love yourself for that care and attention. You will accept your need to pursue your own interests even if it means spending less time with others. Doing something for yourself, say on a weekend, will be seen as natural, congruent, and sensible, as opposed to sitting around drinking endless cups of coffee when you would really rather be doing something else. The bumper stickers you see everywhere, "I'd rather be sailing (hiking, reading, golfing)", will change to, "I'm doing what I want now!"

You'll spend less time frittering away the day on excuses, sidetracks, diversions, and procrastinations. You'll go directly to what you want. You will start to live through yourself rather than through others. You'll take healthy risks, break out of old patterns and ruts, because you are no longer dependent on people, substances or distractions for fulfillment.

You'll be much happier at home because you will know how to negotiate a relationship according to the mission you are here to fulfill. Instead of choosing someone on whom you are dependent, you'll make choices based on how your dreams will be realized. If a relationship is not conducive to your growth, you will have the courage and wisdom to sever it lovingly and promptly.

You will recognize that long relationships must produce a fulfilling and growth-producing environment and nothing else. People will negotiate with each other out of true desire, rather than what they are supposed to want.

Can you add to this list?

268

Vade Mecum *(Go with Me)*

And now, dear reader, it is time for some closing remarks to accompany you beyond this book:

1. You are not alone. No matter what your situation, whether you are in a relationship, a single parent, living alone, divorced or widowed, all your inner work is in partnership, collaboration, and cooperation with your Source. It's a duo. Your Source stays with you even when the going gets rough. In fact, for all the roughing up you do to your Source, it is amazing to think of its resilience, loyalty, and perseverance. You must think of it as the protector of your well-being, the wise silent observer, the nurturer of your talents, the channel for your good.

You need only to listen to a Bach chorale, see a Gothic cathedral, work on a computer, or admire a poem by Emily Dickinson to realize that a Source is operative in their creations—indeed in all creations. It is also in you.

Much in the twentieth century has enticed us away from a feeling of spiritual support. There is indeed something beyond you, as well as in you, which supports and protects your being. You are actually a part of this creative Source, not separated from it in a sort of I-Thou dichotomy.

Your energy comes from your Source. When you are creative, you give this energy back to the universe in an ever-flowing cycle. What is divine in you is both an expression of your own Source, and a reflection of the spiritual energy radiating out from a central place. It is both you and not you. That's the paradox.

2. Trust your path. The paradox continues. You have only one task to perform in this life: being yourself. It's momentous yet simple. You are charged with fulfilling the unique role you have been called to perform.

No Virginia—or Virgil—this is not selfishness! It's the most responsible thing you can do for yourself. Much of the unhappiness in the world is caused by placing demands on others rather that fulfilling one's own needs. You will find that when you commit to your role, you will contribute more to others, to society, and to the world at large.

3. Keep on keeping on. The old adage is "nothing succeeds like success." But success is often a string of failures dared to be experienced. Success actually comes from perseverance: not the bang-your-head-against-the-wall type of keeping on, but the type where you try again another way, a creative way.

As the gallery of clients presented to you in this book has illustrated, you must affirm your path, say yes to what you need, and NO to those who would keep you from it.

4. Exercise rigorous self-honesty. Never lie to yourself about who you are or how you want to express yourself. A con job on yourself sentences you to imprisonment within a stranger. Don't spend your life with someone you are not! Be honest, faithful, and devoted to expressing who you are designed to be. Be devoted to yourself, to your calling, and to your mission.

5. No Big Deal: do it yourself. This book has given you exercises, signs, appeals, admonitions, encouragement, examples, and steps to make you trust the process that you alone must carry out. But, take it easy. Stamp the process with a great big NBD: NO

BIG DEAL. Each step is only a mosaic tile in the bigger picture. "Life is just a bowl of cherries" as the lyric says.

6. Embrace your desires. Part of finding your Life Mission is to acknowledge the desires that you feel and affirm them daily. Somehow people have gotten the message that being desirous of something is suspect. Schiller, the great eighteenth-century German poet, once said that true freedom resulted from fusing what one wants to do with what one must do. Imagine living each day knowing you want to do what you must!

7. Spread the good news. Motivate others to follow their path. Encourage them toward their goals by making positive and supportive comments. I remember one client who clearly identified what she wanted to do, only to have her partner bristle and throw barbs the minute she even talked about it. The partner had a path in mind—hers! The client never regained her courage to complete the process. The more you begin to spread the good news of self-actualization and self-fulfillment and the more you exemplify these values in your life, the more you will further your own journey.

8. Love yourself. Finally, the simplest way to answer your call is to love yourself. This is what you are all about, what you have been created to express, and what you are here to be. The greatest love for yourself is to fulfill your dream, accept your path, carry out your vision, and love the gift you have been endowed with. Remember, you are called to do something which is entirely within your capability, interest, and talent to do!

Love the mission that you have set for yourself, for in the final analysis it is your gift, your challenge to

271

you, your commitment to you. Your mission is love. Embrace it as you would a loved one, and it will return that love with abundance and joy.

Your mission is the talent and sending, the light which shines within you which must be revealed. Enlightenment will be the inevitable result. Illuminate your path, accept and follow it, and your life will be congruent, focused, successful, and authentic. Trust that you are guided and protected during this journey.

You'll discover when you answer the call of your Source that it will permeate everything you do. As a stonemason expressed it in Studs Terkel's book *Working*: "Stone's my life. I daydream all the time most time it's on stone. Oh, I'm gonna build me a stone cabin down on Green River. I'm gonna build stone cabinets in the kitchen. . . . All my dreams, it seems like it's got to have a piece of rock mixed in it."

Another mason named Michelangelo picked out a block of marble in the quarries near Florence. When he found the block he wanted, he immediately began chipping away at it. "What are you doing?" cried one of the quarry workers nearby. "I'm looking for the angel within," Michelangelo replied.

Find your angel within.

Suggested Reading

In addition to the works cited in the acknowledgments, a few more are included for further reading.

Bingen, Hildegard. *Illuminations of Hildegard of Bingen.* Commentary by Matthew Fox. Santa Fe: Bear and Co., 1985.

Bloomfield, Harold, and Kory, Robert. *Inner Joy.* New York: Playboy Paperbacks, 1982.

Bolton, Robert, and Bolton, Dorothy Grover. *Social Style/ Management Style.* New York: Amacom, 1984.

Cousins, Norman. *Anatomy of an Illness.* New York: Bantam, 1981.

De Bono, E. *Lateral Thinking.* New York: Harper & Row, 1970.

Each Day a New Beginning. Center City, MN: Hazelden Foundation, 1982.

Edwards, Betty. *Drawing on the Right Side of the Brain.* Los Angeles: J. P. Tarcher, Inc., 1979.

Fisher, Richard. *Fisher's Brain Games.* New York: Schocken Books, 1982.

Garfield, Charles. *Peak Performers: The New Heroes of American Business.* New York: Avon Books, 1987.

Hamel, Peter Michael. *Through Music to the Self.* Boulder, CO: Shambhala, 1979.

Lakein, Alan. *How to Get Control of Your Time and Your Life.* New York: New American Library, 1973.

Litvak, Stuart. *Use Your Head.* Englewood Cliffs, N.J.: Prentice-Hall, 1982.

Masters, Robert, and Houston, Jean. *Listening to the Body.* New York: Delta, 1978.

May, Rollo. *The Courage To Create.* New York: Bantam, 1980.

Myers, Isabel Briggs. *Gifts Differing.* Palo Alto: Consulting Psychologists Press, 1980.

Ponder, Catherine. *The Dynamic Laws of Prosperity.* Englewood Cliffs, N.J.: Prentice-Hall, Inc., 1962.

Ray, Michael, and Myers, Rochelle. *Creativity in Business.* Garden City, NY: Doubleday & Company, 1986.

Raudsepp, Eugene, with George P. Hough, Jr. *Creative Growth Games.* New York: Jove Publications, Inc., 1979.

Raudsepp, Eugene. *How Creative Are You?* New York: Perigee Books, 1981.

Restak, Richard. *The Brain: The Last Frontier.* New York: Warner Books, 1979.

Rothenburg, Albert, and Carol R. Hausman, (eds.). *The Creativity Question.* Durham, N.C.: Duke University Press, 1981.

Schaef, Anne Wilson. *When Society Becomes an Addict.* New York: Harper & Row, 1987.

Sher, Barbara. *Wishcraft : How to Get What You Really Want.* New York: Ballantine Books, 1979.

Sinetar, Marsha. *Do What You Want: The Money Will Follow.* New York: Paulist Press, 1987.

Steinem, Gloria. *Outrageous Acts and Everyday Rebellions.* New York: New American Library, 1986.

Van Gundy, Arthur B. *Training Your Creative Mind.* Englewood Cliffs, N.J.: Prentice-Hall, Inc., 1982.

Vaughan, Frances. *Awakening Intuition.* Garden City, NY: Anchor Books, 1979.

Van Oech, Roger. *A Whack on the Side of the Head.* New York: Warner Books, 1983.

Yogananda, Paramahansa. *The Autobiography of a Yogi.* Los Angeles: Self-Realization Fellowship, 1956.

Zdenek, Marilee. *The Right Brain Experience.* New York: McGraw-Hill Book Company, 1983.